Abdelaziz Bouchara

Politeness in Shakespeare: Applying Brown and Levinson´s politeness theory to Shakespeare's comedies

Diplomica® Verlag GmbH

Bouchara, Abdelaziz: Politeness in Shakespeare: Applying Brown and Levinson´s politeness theory to Shakespeare's comedies, Hamburg, Diplomica Verlag GmbH 2009

ISBN: 978-3-8366-7753-0
Druck Diplomica® Verlag GmbH, Hamburg, 2009

Bibliografische Information der Deutschen Bibliothek
Die Deutsche Bibliothek verzeichnet diese Publikation in der Deutschen Nationalbibliografie;
detaillierte bibliografische Daten sind im Internet über
<http://dnb.ddb.de> abrufbar.

Die digitale Ausgabe (eBook-Ausgabe) dieses Titels trägt die ISBN 978-3-8366-2753-5 und kann über den Handel oder den Verlag bezogen werden.

Dieses Werk ist urheberrechtlich geschützt. Die dadurch begründeten Rechte, insbesondere die der Übersetzung, des Nachdrucks, des Vortrags, der Entnahme von Abbildungen und Tabellen, der Funksendung, der Mikroverfilmung oder der Vervielfältigung auf anderen Wegen und der Speicherung in Datenverarbeitungsanlagen, bleiben, auch bei nur auszugsweiser Verwertung, vorbehalten. Eine Vervielfältigung dieses Werkes oder von Teilen dieses Werkes ist auch im Einzelfall nur in den Grenzen der gesetzlichen Bestimmungen des Urheberrechtsgesetzes der Bundesrepublik Deutschland in der jeweils geltenden Fassung zulässig. Sie ist grundsätzlich vergütungspflichtig. Zuwiderhandlungen unterliegen den Strafbestimmungen des Urheberrechtes.

Die Wiedergabe von Gebrauchsnamen, Handelsnamen, Warenbezeichnungen usw. in diesem Werk berechtigt auch ohne besondere Kennzeichnung nicht zu der Annahme, dass solche Namen im Sinne der Warenzeichen- und Markenschutz-Gesetzgebung als frei zu betrachten wären und daher von jedermann benutzt werden dürften.

Die Informationen in diesem Werk wurden mit Sorgfalt erarbeitet. Dennoch können Fehler nicht vollständig ausgeschlossen werden und der Verlag, die Autoren oder Übersetzer übernehmen keine juristische Verantwortung oder irgendeine Haftung für evtl. verbliebene fehlerhafte Angaben und deren Folgen.

© Diplomica Verlag GmbH
http://www.diplomica-verlag.de, Hamburg 2009
Printed in Germany

Table of Contents

	Pages
Abbreviations	3
1 Introduction	5
2 The Brown and Levinson model: some central concepts	8
2.1 Face	8
2.1.1 Face-work	8
2.1.2 Positive and negative face	8
2.1.3 Face-threatening acts	9
2.2 Strategies for carrying face-threatening acts	9
2.2.1 Bald on-record	10
2.2.2 Positive and negative politeness	11
2.2.3 Off-record	12
2.3 The social context: power, distance, and ranked extremity	13
2.4 Summary	14
3 Politeness theory and literary discourse	15
3.1 The Brown/Gilman version of the Brown/Levinson model	16
3.2 Politeness theory and Shakespeare´s dramas	21
3.2.1 The scoring of deference	21
3.2.2 Unscored face-threatening acts	23
3.2.3. Applying the model to Shakespeare´s four major tragedies	27
3.2.3.1 Power	27
3.2.3.2 Extremity	28
3.2.3.3 Distance	29
4 Applying the model to four Shakespearean comedies	30
4.1 Power	30
4.1.1 Contrasts confirming the theory	31
4.1.2 Contrasts contradicting the theory	54
4.1.2.1 Strongly contradictory contrasts	54
4.1.2.2 Weakly contradictory contrasts	58
4.2 Extremity	59
4.3 Distance	75
4.3.1 Some consequences of the relationship affect variable	76
4.3.2 Contrasts of distance as affect	78
5 Conclusion	89
6 References	92
Appendix	94

Abbreviations

FTA	face-threatening act
S	speaker
H	hearer
P	power
D	distance
Rx	rating of imposition
Wx	seriousness (weightiness) of FTA x

1 Introduction

The aim of this study is to analyse four historical texts with the help of the parameters of politeness provided by Brown and Levinson (1978) along the lines proposed by Brown and Gilman (1989). Shakespeare's four comedies *Much Ado about Nothing, Measure for Measure, The Taming of the Shrew,* and *Twelfth Night* were chosen in contrast with Brown and Gilman's treatment of four major tragedies *Hamlet, King Lear, Macbeth,* and *Othello*. It was hoped to see whether the comedy setting would yield different results than the tragedy genre. Because of the limited time space, it was not possible to analyse all the comedies. However, the four comedies chosen represent a wide range of Shakespeare's comic oeuvre, ranging from the early 'light-hearted' *The Taming of the Shrew* (around 1590, cf. Thompson 1984, 3) through the 'mature' *Twelfth Night* to the more 'sombre' *Much Ado about Nothing* and the 'problem play' *Measure for Measure,* which has given rise to a debate on its genre classification, the term 'problem play' deriving from the fact that there are "plays which critics and performers have found difficult to classify under the standard genres of comedy, history, and tragedy [...]. The 'problem plays' occur when the values of tragedy are applied to the problems of comedy" (Fox 1988, 146-47). It will therefore be interesting to see whether the treatment of the variables power, rank, and distance in *Measure for Measure* rather tends towards tragedy or comedy.

The Brown and Levinson model offers a tool to describe the quality of social relationships; thus, it can serve as a discourse framework, for instance, in the analysis of literary dialogue since it enables the analyst to explore, in a systematic way, the relation between language use and the social relationships between the speakers. This is what Roger Brown and Albert Gilman did in their article "Politeness theory and Shakespeare's tragedies". They used drama as their 'data set' to test the applicability of Brown and Levinson's theory to Early Modern English because plays reflect the colloquial spoken language of the time. Moreover, the 'psychological soliloquies' in drama provide access to the inner life of the speakers.

The first introductory chapter will provide a description of the major components of Brown and Levinson's theory of politeness. First, some of the important work by Brown and Levinson will be summarised, relevant terms and categories from their model will be introduced, and the different sort of strategies speakers may use in a variety of verbal acts will be outlined, ranging from commands and complaints to compliments and offers. It will also be explained how the choice of a particular strategy - polite or impolite - is constrained by important contextual factors relating to both speaker and hearer. They include the interactants' relative power (P), their relative social distance (D), and the ranked extremity (R) of the 'face-threatening act', i.e. an act which 'intrinsically' threatens face. The ranked extremity refers to the precise nature of the imposition being made and will form an important constraint: the greater the imposition, the greater the use of politeness.

After giving an outline of the components of the Brown/Levinson model, the Brown/Gilman version of it will be presented, which aims at reducing the number of strategies governing politeness behaviour. Brown and Gilman's procedure will be demonstrated in their application of the modified version to Shakespeare's four major tragedies, *Hamlet*, *King Lear*, *Macbeth*, and *Othello*, by a systematic search for minimal pairs where the dimensions of contrast are power (P), distance (D), and the 'intrinsic' extremity (R) of the 'face-threatening act'. Brown and Gilman put forward a system of scoring, which ranges from -1 to +2, depending on the degree of politeness of a character's linguistic behaviour. After dealing with the scoring of deference, it will be shown why some 'face-threatening acts' do not lend themselves to be integrated in the scoring system. The second chapter will end with a section summarising the outcomes of Brown and Gilman's application of Brown and Levinson's modified model to the four tragedies.

The third chapter, which forms the core of this study, consists of a detailed analysis of 80 minimal pairs, each containing two passages which form a contrast of politeness. The entry forms in the third chapter refer to the appendix where the passages to be analysed are listed. Parentheses immediately after the speech headings identify material not in the original but added as a contextual aid (cf. Brown and Gilman 1989, 208, n: 2). Likewise, brackets take the place of footnotes from the cited edition to clarify terms and constructions relevant to the politeness level of a speech (Ibid., n: 3). The analysis of the three variables is arranged as follows: (1) power (P), (2) rank (R), and (3) distance (D). For ease of exposition, each section is preceded by a table providing the numbers of minimal pairs to be discussed, and the totals are arranged in a descending order. Within the three groups, contrasts congruent with the theory will precede the ones which are incongruent. In analysing the three variables, the succession of the four comedies will be as follows: *Much Ado about Nothing, Measure for Measure, The Taming of the Shrew,* and *Twelfth Night*. The edition quoted from is *The New Cambridge Shakespeare*: *Much Ado about Nothing* (Mares 1988), *Measure for Measure* (Gibbons 1991), *The Taming of the Shrew* (Thompson 1984), and *Twelfth Night* (Donno 1985). The conclusion will mainly compare my results concerning the application of Brown and Levinson's politeness theory to the four comedies with Brown and Gilman's outcomes regarding the four tragedies.

2 The Brown and Levinson model: some central concepts

2.1 Face

2.1.1 Face-work

'Face' is something that can be lost, maintained, or enhanced. "Every person lives in a world of social encounters, involving him either in face-to-face or mediated contact with other participants [...]. The term face may be defined as the positive social value a person effectively claims for himself by the line others assume he has taken during a particular contact" (Goffman 1967, 5). It is generally in every participant's interest to maintain each others' 'face': "The combined effect of the rule of self-respect and the rule of the considerateness is that the person tends to conduct himself during an encounter so as to maintain both his own face and the face of other participants" (ibid.). The actions by means of which people cooperate in maintaining face are called 'face-work'.

2.1.2 Positive and negative face

Brown and Levinson's description of polite interaction goes hand in hand with Goffman's conception of 'face'[1]. They assume that 'face' consists of two related aspects, called positive and negative 'face'. 'Positive face' refers to the positive consistent 'self-image' or personality claimed by interactants, including the desire that others appreciate and approve of this image. 'Negative face', on the other hand, refers to any speaker's right not to be imposed upon and the right to be independent of the social world. The two components of 'face' may be condensed as follows:

---

[1] The notions and labels for positive and negative face derive ultimately from Durkheim's "positive and negative rites" (in The Elementary Forms of Religious Life, 1915), partially via Goffman (cf. Brown and Levinson 1989, 285, n: 8).

"negative face: the want of every 'competent adult member' that his actions be unimpeded by others. Positive face: the want of every member that his wants be desirable to at least some others" (Brown and Levinson 1987, 62).

2.1.3 Face-threatening acts

Brown and Levinson argue that the most commonplace speech acts negotiated in everyday conversation, such as advising, promising, inviting, requesting, ordering, criticising, even complementing, carry an element of risk, for they threaten the "public self-image that every member of a society wants to claim for himself" (1987, 61). It is thus clear that there are acts that do not satisfy the 'face wants' of the addressee and/or the speaker. For instance, asking someone for the loan of his or her car, or requesting some similar service is clearly an imposition on that person. Such requests threaten the 'negative face' of the addressee, encroaching on his or her desire to be free from imposition. Other acts, such as the use of insults and terms of abuse, pose a different threat. Calling someone a 'silly ass' clearly demonstrates an unfavourable evaluation of the hearer's 'public self-image' and can thus be regarded as a threat to the latter's 'positive face'. Acts which threaten either the positive or the negative 'face' of the addressee are called 'face-threatening acts' (hereafter abbreviated to FTAs).

2.2 Strategies for carrying face-threatening acts

It goes without saying that speakers who want to reach their aims cannot do without FTAs. Politeness, as Brown and Levinson define it, consists of a set of strategies that serve to minimise the risks to 'face' or 'self-esteem' whenever a speaker commits a 'face-threatening act'. Their argument is that politeness strategies follow from the human ability to reason and find means to achieve one's ends. The question is how to perform the FTAs. There are various ways, depending on the context of interaction, the social relationship of the speakers and the amount of imposition which the FTA entails. To carry out an FTA, a speaker may select one of the four following strategies. They are ordered here from most to least threatening.

2.2.1 Bald on-record

'Bald on-record' conforms with Grice´s Maxims. Grice (1975) claims that people entering into conversation with each other tacitly agree to co-operate towards mutual communicative ends. He calls these conventions maxims and suggests that at least the following four obtain:

- Maxim of quality: Be non-spurious (speak the truth, be sincere)
- Maxim of quantity:
  (a) Don´t say less than is required
  (b) Don´t say more than is required
- Maxim of Relevance: Be relevant
- Maxim of manner: Avoid ambiguity and obscurity
  (Brown and Levinson 1987, 95)

These maxims fall under the so-called 'cooperative principle', i.e. "Make your conversational contribution such as is required, at the stage at which it occurs, by the accepted purpose or direction of the talk exchange in which you are engaged" (Grice 1975, 67). Whenever speakers want to do FTAs with maximum efficiency, they will choose the strategy 'bald on-record'. In such a case, the communicative intention that led a certain actor to do a certain act is clear. During an operation, for instance, utterances like 'help!', 'watch out', etc. are used totally without redress, as this would decrease the urgency that is being communicated.

2.2.2 Positive and negative politeness

'Positive politeness' asserts identification between participants and is meant to meet 'positive face' needs (cf. Brown/Gilman 1987, 162). The phrase 'have a good day' is an example of 'positive politeness'; the speaker wishes for the hearer what the hearer wishes for himself. The verbal repertoire involved here is like the verbal behaviour between friends: "make A feel good - be friendly" (Lakoff 1973, 298). This strategy is understood as a strategy of intimacy.

"Negative politeness is defined as any attempt to meet negative face wants" (Brown/Gilman 1987, 162). Unlike 'positive politeness' it increases social distance. For instance, someone might be requested to close a door in the following way: 'would you mind closing the door ?'. By choosing to perform the FTA with redressive action, the speaker gives redress to the hearer's desire for self-determination and freedom from imposition. As the above example redresses the hearer's 'negative face', it can be said to be an instance of negative politeness.

The terms 'positive politeness' and 'negative politeness' are confusing, i.e. the first one seems to have a positive connotation and the second a negative one. That is why other authors (cf. Scollon and Scollon 1983, 166-8) prefer 'deference politeness' for 'negative politeness' and 'solidarity politeness' for 'positive politeness'. They argue that deference is the essence of 'negative politeness', and they maintain that by choosing the term 'solidarity' the emphasis on the 'common grounds' of the relation of the participants is more evident. However, 'positive politeness' and 'negative politeness' are used throughout in this study because of the adoption of the Brown/Levinson model.

2.2.3 Off-record

'Off-record' utterances are indirect uses of language whose precise meaning has to be interpreted. A number of off-record strategies may lead to the violation of Grice's conversational maxims:

a. The Maxim of Relevance is violated if a speaker says something that is not explicitly relevant. The utterance 'this soup is a bit bland' implies 'pass the salt' and violates the Relevance Maxim (cf. Brown and Levinson 1987, 215).

b. Being indirect, a speaker inevitably violates the Maxim of Quantity. This may be done by exaggerating, : 'I tried to call a hundred times, but there was never any answer' (ibid., 219).

c. The violation of the Maxim of Quality is reflected, for instance, in figures of speech, such as irony and metaphor, which lead the hearer to find some implicature[2] for the intended message. By being ironic a speaker can convey his meaning indirectly, cf. 'beautiful weather, isn't it! (to postman drenched in rainstorm)' (ibid., 222).

d. By being vague or ambiguous, a speaker violates the Maxim of Manner or Modality and invites no particular implicatures. Ambiguities produce vagueness and thus minimise the threats. "'John's a pretty sharp/smooth cookie' could be either a compliment or an insult, depending on which of the connotations of *sharp* or *smooth* are latched on to" (ibid., 225).

As the above examples show, the 'off-record' strategies go beyond 'negative politeness' because they imply a higher degree of indirectness.

---

[2] Grice coined the term 'implicature' for indirect, context-determined meaning (cf. Short 1989, 150).

2.3 The social context: power, distance, and ranked extremity

In trying to define the principles of polite speech, Brown and Levinson (1987) propose that the choice of a particular strategy - whether it is polite or impolite - is constrained by important contextual factors relating to both speaker and hearer. These contextual factors include the ranking of the imposition of the act itself (e.g. asking for the time is less imposing than asking for a loan), the relative power of the hearer over the speaker, and the social distance between speaker and hearer. According to Brown and Levinson, these constraints, which are the universal determinants of politeness levels in speech acts, specify the particular verbal strategy employed to accomplish the repair work of politeness. Hence, a speaker's choice of which strategy to use is a function of the threat implied by the intended act (termed its 'weightiness'). Brown and Levinson (1987, 76) suggest the formula

$$Wx = D(S, H) + P(H, S) + Rx$$

where Wx refers to the 'weightiness' of the FTA, D(S,H) to the distance between speaker and hearer, P(H,S) to the power of the hearer over the speaker, and Rx to the degree of imposition of the act. To clarify this point, let us consider each variable in turn:

> with P and R held constant and small, only the expression of D varies in the following two sentences:
> (1) Excuse me, would you by any chance have the time?
> (2) Got the time, mate?
> Our intuitions are that (1) would be used where (in S's perception) S and H were distant (strangers from different parts, say), and (2) where S and H were close (either known to each other, or perceptibly 'similar' in social terms). D, then, is the only variable in our formula that changes from (1) to (2), and in doing so lessens Wx [...].
> Turning to the P variable, suppose D and R are held constant and have small values [...]:
> (3) Excuse me sir, would it be all right if I smoke?
> (4) Mind if I smoke?

Our intuitions are that (3) might be said by an employee to his boss, while (4) might be said by the boss to the employee in the same situation. Here, then, P is the only variable that changes from (3) to (4) (more exactly, P of H over S) [...].

That R is also independently variable can be similarly demonstrated. Suppose P is small and D is great (S and H are strangers, for example), and P and R are held constant. Then compare:

(5) Look, I'm terribly sorry to bother you but would there be any chance of your lending me just enough money to get a railway ticket to get home? I must have dropped my purse and I just don't know what to do.

(6) Hey, got change for a quarter?

Both might be said at a railway station by a frustrated traveller to a stranger, but our intuitions are that S in saying (5) considers the FTA to be much more serious than the FTA done in (6). The only variable is R, and it must be because Rx is lower in (6) that the language appropriate to a low Wx is employed there (Brown and Levinson 1987, 80-81).

Clearly enough, P(ower), D(istance), and R(ank) are crucial in determining the level of politeness which a speaker will use.

2.4 Summary

The more an act threatens the speaker or hearer's face, the more the speaker wants to choose a 'higher-numbered' strategy. The choice may be schematised as follows:

Circumstances determining choice of strategy

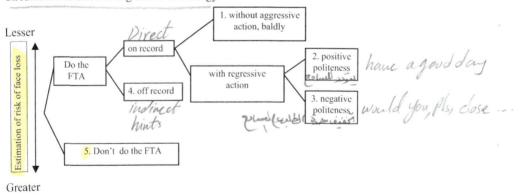

Fig. 1: Super-strategies of politeness ordered against estimated risk of face loss (Brown and Levinson 1987, 60)

Each strategy on the scheme is numbered; the higher the number, the more polite the strategy. Clearly, strategy (5), which avoids the FTA altogether, represents no imposition at all. Silence may be adopted when the FTA is too dangerous to commit. 'Better not to speak than to be sorry' is the understanding behind it. Strategy (4) is the 'off-record' realisation of an FTA; it includes "metaphor and irony, rhetorical questions, understatement, tautologies, all kinds of hints [...] so that the meaning is to some degree negotiable" (Brown and Levinson 1987, 69). In other words, the hearer is given considerable choice of interpretation because the intended function of the FTA is 'obscured'. Strategy (1), which is maximally direct, incorporates no politeness markers at all. It is used, for instance, when the speaker holds a position of high relative power over the hearer and fears no serious consequences from using such a strategy. Between the two extremes, Brown and Levinson position their main politeness 'super-strategies': positive and negative politeness strategies. Positive politeness strategies are representative of the linguistic behaviour between intimates and are meant to address the hearer's wish for approval. They are also used to imply, among other things, 'common ground' even between strangers who share the same purpose of interaction. In using these strategies the speaker indicates that he or she wants to come closer to the hearer. Negative politeness strategies, on the other hand, address the hearer's wish for non-interference. They are linguistic realisations whose function is to minimise the 'weightiness' of the FTA.

3 Politeness theory and literary discourse

In "Politeness theory and Shakespeare's four major tragedies" Roger Brown and Albert Gilman (1989), using a modified version of the Brown/Levinson model, attempted to determine whether the Brown/Levinson claim holds for Shakespeare's Early Modern English in *Hamlet*, *Macbeth*, *King Lear*, and *Othello*. They searched for pairs of minimally contrasting dyads where the dimensions of contrast are P(ower), D(istance), and R(ank). Two speeches involving the same two characters are matched with respect to one of the three variables, and the result is compared to the predictions of politeness theory, i.e. either confirming or contradicting it.

3.1 The Brown/Gilman version of the Brown/Levinson model

The Brown/Gilman version of the Brown/Levinson theory is graphically represented in Fig. 2 below. Two differences can be noticed. The first one concerns the number of strategies used. In the original Brown/Levinson theory, there are five 'super-strategies', whereas in the modified version there are only four. Strategy (2) is, in the original, divided into (2): do the FTA on-record with redressive action (negative politeness), and (3): do the FTA on-record with

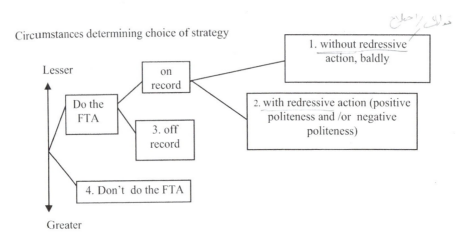

Fig. 2: Substrategies of politeness model ordered against estimated risk of face loss: the modified version (Brown and Gilman 1989, 165)

redressive action (positive politeness). The modified version, on the contrary, "substitutes a single super-strategy of redress in which acts of positive and negative politeness may be mixed but need not be" (Brown and Gilman 1989,

165). The second difference regards the 'few-many' scale between (1) and (2). This means that when an FTA is redressed, "the amount of redress, the number of codable substrategies, will increase (from few to many) as the estimated risk of face loss or weightiness (Wx) increases" (Ibid., 166). Brown and Gilman illustrate the 15 subtrategies of positive politeness (cf. Table 1 below) and the ten substrategies of negative politeness (cf. Table 2 below) with examples from Shakespeare.

As Table 1 illustrates, positive politeness strategies are oriented towards the positive 'face' of the hearer. They involve three mechanisms, labelled 1 to 15 (cf. Brown and Levinson 1987, 102). Those of the first type (1-8) involve the speaker's claim of 'common ground' with the hearer. Three ways of making this claim are illustrated by examples (1-3): the speaker may convey that some of the hearer's goals or desired object are admirable or interesting to the speaker too; or the speaker may stress a 'common membership' in a group or category (4). Likewise, the speaker can claim a 'common perspective' with the hearer without necessarily referring to 'in-group membership' (5-8). The second major class of positive politeness strategies (9-14) derives from the 'want' to convey that the speaker and the addressee are cooperatively involved in the relevant activity. This cooperation may be stressed by the speakers' indicating their knowledge and sensitivity to the hearers' 'wants', i.e. the satisfaction of their desires (9). It may also be done by claiming some reflexivity to the hearers' 'wants' (10-13). Thirdly, speakers may convey their cooperation with the hearers by indicating the importance of reciprocity and mutual helping (14). Finally, speakers may satisfy the hearers' positive face 'want' by actually fulfilling some of

Identify the speech, addresser and addressee and analyze the power, distance and ranked ex[tent].

1. Notice admirable qualities, possessions, etc.
   First Senator. Adieu, brave Moor. (Othello, 1, III, 286)
   Desdemona: Alas, thrice-gentle Cassio. (Othello, 111, Iv, 122)
2. Exaggerate sympathy, approval, etc.
   Goneril (to King Lear): A love that makes breath poor, and speech unable:
   Beyond all manner of so much 1 love you. (King Lear, 1, I, 62-63)
   Regan (to King Lear): And find I am alone felicitate
   In your dear Highness'love. (King Lear, 1, I, 77-78)
3. Intensify the interest of the hearer in the speaker's contribution.
   Othello (to the Duke and others): And of the Cannibals that each other eat, The Anthropophagi, and men whose heads
   Grew beneath their shoulders. (Othello, 1, III, 142-144)
4. Use in-group identity markers in speech.
   Hamlet (to Horatio)- Sir, my good friend, I'll change that name with you. (1, II, 163)
5. Seek agreement in safe topics. Edgar (to Edmund): How now, brother Edmund; what serious contemplation are you in? (King Lear, 1, II, 149-150)
6. Avoid possible disagreement by hedging your statements.
   Knight (to King Lear): My lord, I know not what the matter is; but to my judgment...
   (I, IV, 57-58)
7. Assert common ground.
   King (to Rosenerantz and Guildenstern of themselves and Hamlet). I entreat you both that, being of so young days brought up with him,
   And sith so neighbored to his youth and havior. (Hamlet, 11, II, 10-12)
8. Joke to put the hearer at ease.
   Macduff (to porter): Was it so late, friend, are you went to bed,
   That you do lie so late? (Macbeth, 11, III, 23-24)
9. Assert knowledge of the hearer's wants and indicate you are taking account of them.
   Regan (to Oswald of himself and Goneril): I know you are of her bosom. (King Lear, IV, v, 26)
10. Offer, promise.
    Regan (to Oswald). I'll love thee much,
    Let me unseal the letter. (King Lear, IV, v, 21-22)
11. Be optimistic that the hearer wants what the speaker wants, that the FTA is slight.
    Desdemona (to Othello of Cassio): How now, my lord?
    I have been talking with a suitor here,
    A man that languishes in your displeasure. (111, III, 41-43)
    Desdemona (to Othello of Cassio): I prithee call him back. (111, III, 51)
    Desdemona (to Othello of Cassio): Why, this is not a boon;
    'Tis as 1 should entreat you wear your gloves. (Othello, 111, III, 76-77)
12. Use an inclusive form to include both speaker and hearer in the activity. *Goneril* (to Regan)-
    Pray you, let's hit [agree] together; if our father carry authority with such disposition as he bears [continues in this frame of mind], this last surrender
    [recent abdication of his will but offend [vex] us. (King Lear, 1, I, 306-309)
13. Give reasons why speaker wants what he or she does so that it will seem reasonable to the hearer.
    Regan (to Edmund): Our troops set forth tomorrow: stay with us,
    The ways are dangerous. (King Lear, IV, v, 16-17)
14. Assert reciprocal exchange or tit for tat.
    Macbeth (to Banquo): If you shall cleave to my consent, when
    'tis [join my cause when the time comes],
    It shall make honor for you. (*Macbeth*, 11, I, 25-26)
15. Give something desired. gifts, position, sympathy, understanding.
    Goneril (to Edmund): Decline your head. This kiss, if it durst speak,
    Would stretch thy spirits up into the air. (King Lear, IV, II, 22-23)

Table 1. Substrategies of positive politeness (Brown and Gilman 1989, 167)

the hearers' 'wants' of gift-giving and "human relations' wants such as [...] the wants to be liked, admired, cared about, understood, listened to, and so on " (Brown and Levinson 1989, 129).

The examples in Table 2 below are forms of social 'distancing' and are oriented towards the negative face of the hearer. They can be divided into three main groups as well (cf. Brown and Levinson 1987, 131). The first type (1-5) mainly involves the speaker's avoidance to coerce the hearer's response, and this may be done by being indirect (1), by carefully avoiding presuming or assuming that anything involved in the FTA is desired or believed by the hearer (2), or by assuming that the hearer is not likely to do the act (3). The avoidance of coerciveness can be further expressed by minimising the threat (4) or making explicit the three 'sociological' variables: power (P), distance (D), and the ranked extremity (R) (5). With regard to the second type, the speaker can either communicate his or her intention not to offend the hearer by apologising for the infringement (6) or by dissociating himself or herself from the particular FTA through the use of mechanisms that distance the speaker from the hearer (7-9). Finally, the speaker can communicate the FTA by explicitly claiming indebtedness to the hearer (10). Tables 1 and 2 are based on Brown and Levinson (1987), but several levels are considerably modified. Brown and Levinson go into considerable detail in their discussion of the strategies listed, providing a comprehensive description of the various strategies that speakers have at their disposal. Bearing in mind the scope of this study it is not possible to deal with the two tables in detail at this stage. Instead, this particular feature has been reserved for the third chapter, which forms the core of this book.

1. Be conventionally indirect.
    Iago (to Othello): You were best go in. (I, ii, 29)
    Banquo: Worthy Macbeth, we stay upon your leisure
    [convenience]. (Othello, iii, 148)
2. Do not assume willingness to comply. Question, hedge.
    Queen (to Rosencrantz and Guildenstern): If it will please you
    To show us so much gentry [courtesy] and good will.
    (Hamlet, II, ii, 21-22)
3. Be pessimistic about ability or willingness to comply. Use the subjunctive.
    Osric (to Hamlet): Sweet lord, if your lordship were at leisure,
    I should impart a thing to you from his Majesty. (Hamlet, V, ii, 91-92)
4. Minimize the imposition.
    Edgar (to Albany): Hear me one word. (King Lear, V, i, 39)
5. Give deference.
    Othello (to the Duke and Venetian Senators). Most potent, grave, and reverend seigniors,
    My very noble and approved good masters. (Othello, I, iii, 76-77)
6. Apologize. Admit the impingement, express reluctance, ask forgiveness.
    Ross (to Macduff)- Let not your ears despise my tongue for ever,
    Which shall possess them with the heaviest sound
    That ever yet they heard. (Macbeth, IV, iii, 201-203)
7. Impersonalize the speaker and hearer. Use the passive without agent.
    Knight (to King Lear). your Highness is not entertained
    With that ceremonious affection
    As you were wont. (King Lear, I, iv, 58-60)
8. State the FTA as an instance of a General rule to soften the offense.
    Gloucester (to King Lear): My dear lord,
    You know the fiery quality of the Duke,
    How unremovable and fixed he is
    In his own course. (King Lear, II, iv, 90-93)
9. Nominalize to distance the actor and add formality.
    King (to Hamlet): But to persevere
    In obstinate condolement is a course
    Of impious stubbornness. (Hamlet, I, ii, 92-94)
10. Go on record as incurring a debt.
    Queen (to Rosencrantz and Guildenstern): Your visitation shall receive such thanks
    As fits a king's remembrance. (Hamlet, II, ii, 25-26)

Table 2. Substrategies of negative politeness (Brown and Gilman 1989, 168)

It is true that the original theory does not include the 'few-many' scale, but Brown and Levinson's remarks suggest that they are aware of this phenomenon. They argue that "[i]n general, the more *effort* S expends in face-maintaining linguistic behaviour, the more S communicates his sincere desire that H's face wants be satisfied [...]. He may achieve this effort simply by compounding the branching means to achieve wants, or by elaborate realizations of particular means, or both" (1987, 93).

3.2 Politeness theory and Shakespeare's dramas

To test politeness theory, the effect of each variable in isolation needed to be known.

> The plan was to find pairs of speeches involving the same two characters such that the relationship between the characters would be the same on the occasions of the two speeches with respect to two out of three weightiness variables (P, D, and R) but clearly different on the third [...]. With attention limited to just the obvious and frequent FTAs, one proceeds a step at a time.
> 1. In each play for each pair of characters, record the first FTA - either positive or negative [...]. The length of the FTA, the amount of text recorded, is defined as all the text necessary to specify the FTA plus all continuous antecedent and subsequent text that does not belong to a new speech act.
> 2. Code the FTA for the three variables defining its intrinsic weightiness: P, D, and R. Power was coded as equal or as hearer higher than speaker, or as speaker higher than hearer [...].
> 3. Score the total speech for politeness. This is done by first identifying the super-strategy employed [...]. When the super-strategy involves redressive action, the speech is scored further by assigning one point for each instance of any of the 15 substrategies of positive politeness and one point for each instance of the 10 substrategies of negative politeness and totalling the points. For two negative politeness strategies involving deference, (1) and (5), a wider scoring range was used: from -1 to +2 [...].
> 4. Search for a second FTA involving the same two characters as the first [...] such that the two FTAs are matched with respect to two out of three of the variables: P, D, R. This kind of near-match often appears very near the first speech but it need not; the near-match may be widely separated in the play as, often, when two characters who are friendly at the start (low D) fall out later on) [...] (Brown and Gilman 1989, 173-4).

3.2.1 The Scoring of deference إذعان

In scoring deference, which is involved in negative politeness (cf. Table 2, sub-strategies (1) and (5), Brown and Gilman took into consideration forms of address (Names and titles and pronouns of address (5)) and the formulation of indirect requests (1). As far as names and titles are concerned, unadorned titles (e.g. *sir, madam, my lord*) and names with one honorific adjective (e.g. *worthy Montano, good Hamlet*) are scored the same way: each scores one point for deference. Titles adorned with honorific adjectives (e.g. *my dread lord, madam, good madam, good your Grace,* etc.) score two points. Brown and Gilman treated the name alone (e.g. *Desdemona, Macbeth*) as the neutral level scoring no points. However, "there is one form that is neither neutral nor deferential but usually depreciative and that is *sirrah*, said to an adult by a person of higher status; to a child, *sirrah* was affectionate" (Brown and Gilman 1989, 176). The use of *sirrah* to an adult caused them to subtract one point (-1).

Concerning pronouns of address, grammars say that *you* was the polite form and *thou* the familiar one. Upper-class speakers said *you* to one another; lower-class speakers addressed each other with *thou*; the between-class rule was *you* to the upper and *thou* to the lower. Brown and Gilman conclude that "[a]n isolated *thou* of contempt scores -1; an isolated deferential *you* scores +1 for negative politeness; and an isolated *thou* of affection scores +1 for positive politeness (strategy (4): Use in-group identity markers)" (1989, 179).

As to indirect requests, there is good evidence (cf. Clark & Schunk 1980) to suggest that hearers process both the literal meaning and the directive or speech act meaning. The directive meaning is needed to identify the response to be made, and the literal meaning is processed to add the politeness. Brown and Gilman (1989) treated *I beseech you* and *I do beseech you* as more deferential than *I pray you*, and they assigned the two indirect requests two points as against one for *I pray you* and *pray you*. *If you please* or *so please you* and *I entreat you* are also scored +2. *Prithee* co-occurs with terms of friendship, affection, and various

Christian names (e.g. *good friend, my son, shepherd*, etc.). It is scored for positive politeness strategy (4): use in-group identity terms. Simple imperatives (*go, come*, etc.) and simple imperatives followed by the second person subject (*go you, retire thee*) are treated both as neutral in that neither scores a point for deference. Finally, verbless imperatives as in *Peace, Kent*! (*King Lear*) and *Thy story quickly* (*Macbeth*) are neither polite nor neutral but 'rudely brusque'. They were scored, like *sirrah*, among forms of address, as -1.

> The full procedure can now be summarized. The four plays were systematically searched for pairs of minimally contrasting discourse dyads where the dimensions of contrast were power (P), distance (D), and the intrinsic extremity of the FTA (R). Whenever such a pair was found, a pair contrasting only in P or only in D or only in R, there would be two speeches to be scored for politeness and a prediction from theory as to which of the two ought to be more polite [...]. In scoring the politeness of a speech, belonging to super-strategy (2), one point (+1) was usually given for each instance of any substrategy, positive or negative. With negative politeness strategy (1) (Be conventionally indirect) and strategy (5) (Give deference) the scores ranged from -1 to +2. The total politeness score for a speech was the sum of its points (Brown and Gilman 1989, 184).

The method might seem simple, but it is, in reality, a serious undertaking since even the authors admit that "the logic is unimpeachable, but in practice it proved impossible to make all the scorings objective and independent" (Brown and Gilman 1989, 173).

3.2.2 Unscored face-threatening acts

"It would not be a fair test of politeness theory to go blindly into the plays scoring every speech that met the criteria of minimal contrast in terms of P, D, or R" (Brown and Gilman 1989, 184). To carry out an FTA with 'maximum efficiency', Shakespeare chooses the bald on-record strategy for his characters. This can be seen, for example, in cases of great urgency, where no face redress is felt to be necessary. However, especially in literary dialogue, cases of non-redressive action happen quite often. They can also be observed in circumstances of rage, drunkenness, and madness. Here every substrategy of positive or negative politeness vanishes.

In states of rage, the characters in question do not pay attention to P, D, and R. The rage scenes are therefore excluded from the scoring because there is no concern for the hearer's face. Hamlet is just in such a state in the following passage where he scornfully reproaches his mother in her closet for sleeping with his father's murderer.

> Nay, but to live
> In the rank sweat of an estimated bed,
> Stewed in corruption, honeying and making love
> Over the nasty sty-
> (3, 4, 92-95)

In the comedies states of rage are also found. In *Measure for Measure*, for instance, Isabella flies into a rage and scolds her brother, Claudio, who, to her dismay, begs her to sleep with Angelo in order to save his head.

> O you beast [because unmanly and devoid of soul]!
> O faithless coward! O dishonest wretch!
> Wilt thou be made a man [given life] out of my vice?
> Is't not a kind of incest, to take life
> From thine own sister's shame? What should I think?
> Heaven shield [ensure] my mother play'd my father fair!
> For such a warped [deformed] slip of wilderness [shoot of wild stock]
> Ne'er issued from his blood. Take my defiance [declaration of contempt]
> Die, perish! Might but my bending down
> Reprieve thee from thy fate, it should proceed:
> I'll pray a thousand prayers for thy death,
> No word to save thee.
> (3, 1, 136-47)

Likewise, drunken characters ignore P, D, and R as well. When Montano, governor of Cyprus, for instance, addresses Cassio, Othello's lieutenant, as follows:

Montano Nay, good lieutenant! I pray you, sir, hold
         your hand

Cassio responds with:

Cassio Let me go, sir, or I'll knock you o'er the
        mazzard [head].
        (2, 3, 148-151)

There is social asymmetry between Montano and Cassio: Cassio is supposed to be more polite than Montano. What happens is quite the opposite because Cassio is drunk, which accounts for his incivility. At the start of the Induction to *The Taming of the Shrew* the hostess indignantly throws the drunken Sly out of her tavern, for refusing to pay all the glasses he has broken. Being drunk he reacts with the following speech, where the hostess is addressed with the contemptuous male term of address 'boy':

Sly Third, or fourth, or fifth borough, I'll answer him
     By law: I'll not budge an inch, boy: let him come,
     and kindly.
     [Falls asleep]
     (Induction 1, 20-21)

Thompson argues that 'boy' "is a contemptuous form of address to a servant or inferior. This is the only example in Shakespeare of it being applied to a woman, so perhaps it is another drunken error" (1984, 4, n: 11). Politeness is wiped out when a speech is produced in a state of drunkenness, and this indifference to the hearer's face makes Brown and Gilman exclude drunkenness in the collecting of minimal pairs.

In madness as well, politeness is eliminated altogether. The feeling for the other is disregarded, and Grice's Maxims are overthrown. In the tragedies, Ophelia's and King Lear's madness, for instance, are excluded from the scoring. In the comedies analysed in this study scenes involving madness are not found. In

Twelfth Night, Malvolio, Olivia's steward, is imprisoned as a madman but the reader knows that he is sane.

It is true that the comedies in question do not exhibit scenes of madness, but *The Taming of the Shrew* displays speeches that cannot be scored either, namely the speeches which involve Christopher Sly, a tinker, who, in the Induction to the play, is tricked into believing that he is a lord, and the success of the deception requires, among other things, that he should be addressed with terms appropriate to a lord. The following contrast will clarify this point:

Second Servant (inviting Sly to wash his hands and making him believe
that he woke from a fifteen-years sleep)
Will't please your mightiness to wash your hands?
O, how we joy to see your wit [intelligence] restored!
O, that once more you knew but what you are!
These fifteen years you have been in a dream;
Or when you waked, so waked as if you slept.
(Induction 2, 72-76)

Sly (wondering at the long period he is made
to believe he was asleep)
These fifteen years! by my fay [faith], a goodly nap.
But did I never speak of [in] all that time?
(Induction 2, 77-78)

Sly's confusion is clearly seen when he is presented with a wife:

Sly (attempting to discover whether he is awake by checking his
senses)
Am I a lord? and have I such a lady?
Or do I dream? or have I dream'd till now?
I do not sleep: I see, I hear, I speak;
I smell sweet savours and I feel soft things:
Upon my life, I am a lord indeed
And not a tinker nor Christophero Sly.
Well, bring our lady hither to our sight;
And once again, a pot o' the smallest ale.
(Induction 2, 64-71)

Sly spends his time bewildered at the attention shown to him or drunkenly enjoying it, and it would be a mistake to compare the pretended politeness enacted in the speeches addressed to him in minimal pairs.

In sum, states of rage, drunkenness, madness as well as the scenes involving Sly (*The Taming of the Shrew*) being addressed as a lord are excluded from the scoring in the hope of achieving a fair test of politeness instead of blindly comparing each speech which has some relevance to the three variables power (P), rank (R), and distance (D).

3. 2. 3 Applying the model to Shakespeare´s four major tragedies

3. 2. 3. 1 Power

To test the effects of the variable power (P), "[t]wo speaker-hearer FTAs are compared for politeness scores. The persons are of clearly different power and they switch roles (speaker and hearer) in the comparison cases, with D and R constant" (Brown and Levinson 1989, 187). Table 3 below shows that *Macbeth* has only one third as many dyads as *King Lear* (7 versus 21) because *Macbeth* is only about two-thirds the length of each of the other three tragedies (cf. Brown and Gilman 1989, 188). *Hamlet* and *Othello* are in between, but the latter has considerably more dyads than the former (17 versus 12). *Hamlet* and *Macbeth* score no strongly contradictory contrasts, while *Othello* is less strongly disconfirming the theory than *King Lear* (1/17 versus 1/7). On the other hand, *King Lear* and *Othello* score no weakly contradictory contrasts, while *Hamlet* scores slightly higher than *Macbeth* (2 versus 1). There are 57 contrasts in the four tragedies, and 50 of them are congruent with the theory, as against four strongly and three weakly contradictory ones. The preponderance of the number of contrasts congruent with the theory supports the hypotheses incorporated in Brown and Levinson´s theory of politeness.

Play	Congruent with theory[a]	Weakly contradictory to theory[b]	Strongly contradictory to theory[c]	Total
King Lear	18	0	3	21
Othello	16	0	1	17
Hamlet	10	2	0	12
Macbeth	6	1	0	7
Total	50	3	4	57

Table 3. Contrasts of power alone (Adapted from Brown and Gilman 1989, 188)
[a] The person with less power is more polite
[b] The two persons of unequal power are equally polite
[c] The person with more power is more polite

3. 2. 3. 2 Extremity

To make a test of the effect of "the extremity of the FTA, a given speaker must make two-face-threatening speeches, of clearly unequal extremity, to a given hearer" (Brown and Gilman 1989, 196). Table 4 shows that *King Lear* has more than twice as many dyads as *Macbeth* and *Othello*. *Hamlet* is in between. Only one contrast weakly disconfirming the theory is found in *Hamlet*. There are 19 contrasts in the four plays, and 18 of them are congruent with the theory. The predictions of politeness theory for the variable rank (R) are thus confirmed.

Play	Congruent with theory[a]	Weakly contradictory to theory[b]	Strongly contradictory to theory[c]	Total
King Lear	8	0	0	8
Hamlet	5	1	0	6
Macbeth	3	0	0	3
Othello	2	0	0	2
Total	18	1	0	19

Table 4. Contrasts of extremity alone (Adapted from Brown and Gilman 1989, 197)
[a] The more extreme face threat is more politely expressed
[b] Two face threats, differing in extremity, are expressed with equal politeness
[c] The more extreme face threat is less politely expressed

3. 2. 3. 3 Distance

In order to test the effects of the variable distance, "we need two FTAs involving the same two persons with each person staying in speaker or hearer role. Power relations must remain the same; the two FTAs must be matched in extremity, but there must be a clear change in D, which could be a change of affection or interactive closeness or both" (Brown and Gilman 1989, 192). In Table 5 distance is interpreted as 'affect', i.e. the more two persons like one another, the greater their concern with protecting each other's face. *Hamlet* and *Othello*, with equal score, have three times as many dyads as *Macbeth* (3 versus 1). *King Lear* is in between (2). There are nine contrasts in the four plays, and all of them strongly contradict Brown and Levinson's predictions for the variable distance in politeness theory.

Brown and Gilman conclude that "politeness in Shakespeare's tragedies increases with the power of the speaker over the hearer and increases with the extremity of the face threat. Politeness decreases with the withdrawal of affection and

Play	Congruent with theory[a]	Weakly contradictory to theory[b]	Strongly contradictory to theory[c]	Total
Hamlet	0	0	3	3
Othello	0	0	3	3
King Lear	0	0	2	2
Macbeth	0	0	1	1
Total	0	0	9	9

Table 5. Contrasts of distance alone with distance interpreted as 'affect' (Adapted from Brown and Gilman 1989, 192)
[a] In the case marked by greater positive affect, speech is less polite
[b] In cases differing in level of politeness positive affect, there is no difference in politeness
[c] In the case marked by greater positive affect, speech is more polite

increases with an increase of affection. The results for power and extremity are those predicted by theory. If affection is thought of as D (or distance) of politeness theory, then the results contradict theory. It is more accurate to say that the affect results call for a reformulation of the D parameter" (1989, 199).

4 Applying the model to four Shakespearean comedies

4.1 Power

To test the effects of the variable power, "[t]wo speaker-hearer FTAs are compared for politeness scores. The persons are of clearly different power and they switch roles (speaker and hearer) in the comparison cases, with D and R constant" (Brown and Levinson 1987, 187). In the selection of 'outcomes' which are minimal contrasts in power (P) only 'the most critically important instances' for a given pair of characters are taken into consideration (ibid., 189). Table 6 shows that *Measure for Measure* has more than twice as many dyads as *Twelfth Night* and *The Taming of the Shrew* (18 versus 8); *Much Ado about Nothing* is in between (12). *Twelfth Night* is most disconfirming the theory (3/8 as against 1/6 for *Much Ado about Nothing* and

Play	Congruent with theory[a]	Weakly contradictory to theory[b]	Strongly contradictory to theory[c]	Total
Measure for Measure	15	1	2	18
Much Ado about Nothing	10	1	1	12
The Taming of the Shrew	7	0	1	8
Twelfth Night	5	1	2	8
Total	37	3	6	46

Table 6. Contrasts of power alone
 [a] The person with less power is more polite
 [b] The two persons of unequal power are equally polite
 [c] The person with more power is more polite

Measure for Measure and 1/8 for *The Taming of the Shrew*). There are 46 contrasts in the plays, and 37 of them are congruent with the theory as against six strongly and three weakly contradictory ones. This is a clear confirmation of the hypotheses incorporated in Brown and Levinson's theory of politeness.

4.1.1 Contrasts confirming the theory

In *Much Ado about Nothing* (1) Leonato, governor of Messilia, addresses Don Pedro, the Duke, with a polite speech befitting a duke. Only negative politeness occurs here: first, the indirect request (*Please it...*) scores +2 for deference. Second, the title *your grace*, which adds another point for deference is, according to Reploge, "proper only for royalty, for dukes and duchesses, and archbishops and their wives" (1973, 183-84). Further deference is observed when Leonato invites Don Pedro to go first (*lead on*: +1), which brings the speech to a total score of +4. Don Pedro's response scores +2 only for positive politeness: +1 for the 'inclusive' *we* and +1 for the 'solidarity' politeness marker *your hand, Leonato*, with which Don Pedro suggests that they go hand in hand. However, Leonato's speech remains more polite than Don Pedro's.

In (2) Don Pedro asks Benedick for the reason why Benedick and Claudio did not want to join the others at Leonato's; his speech scores no points for politeness. The answer would satisfy his curiosity; however, Benedick does not want to disclose Claudio's secret: his falling in love with Hero. Benedick is, in fact, in a dilemma, but his allegiance to the prince leads him to employ polite strategies to mitigate his excuse. The deferential title *your grace* scores +1, and the use of the subjunctive *would*, used twice, to indicate scepticism adds two points, which produces a total score of +3 for negative politeness. Benedick is more polite than Don Pedro.

In (3) Don John, Don Pedro's bastard brother, broods on revenge after his defeat by Don Pedro, in battle. In particular, he plots to 'cross' Claudio, the 'young start-up', who "hath all the glory of my overthrow" (1, 3, 47-50). The FTA which Don John has in mind is too extreme, but he is not concerned about softening the impact of his FTA by using polite markers. He merely wants to know whether he can count on the assistance of his servants in his conspiracy to disgrace Claudio's fiancée, Hero. Conrade's response is characterised by his total devotion to his master. It scores +1 for exaggeration *to the death* and another point for deference *my lord* (negative politeness), which brings the speech to a total score of +2. Conrade is more polite than Don John.

In (4) Don Pedro asks Beatrice, Leonato's niece, whether she would accept him as a husband. The deferential title *lady* scores +1 for negative politeness. In her response, "Beatrice sidesteps Don Pedro's question: he is too good for her, like Sunday clothes on a working day" (Marres 1988, 77, n: 249-50). In doing so, she shows deference by explicitly abasing herself (+1). The deferential titles *my lord* and *your grace*, the latter used twice, score +3, the indirect request *I beseech you* adds +2, begging forgiveness *Pardon me* another point. Beatrice further supplements her politeness by utilising a sub-strategy of apologising (cf. Brown and Levinson 1987, 189): she attempts to state the 'overwhelming reasons', which lead her to perform her FTA (*I was born to speak all mirth and no matter*: +1). This gives a total score of +8 only for negative politeness. Beatrice is more polite than Don Pedro.

In (5) Benedick's order to his servant scores no points for politeness. His servant implicitly promises to perform Benedick's command (positive politeness), which scores +1. The boy's statement *here already* means that he will be back immediately and thereby exaggerates his fulfilment of the order, which adds another point to positive politeness. Furthermore, the deferential title *sir* scores +1 for negative politeness, which brings the speech to a total score of +3. Benedick is less polite than his servant.

In (6) Hero plans to play a trick on Beatrice by letting her overhear how much Benedick loves her. Her speech scores +1 for the positive politeness hedge in *good Margaret*; otherwise, the speech displays a number of directives which are uttered baldly on-record (*run, whisper, say, bid, bear*). Margaret's response to Hero's successive imperatives scores +1 because she implicitly promises to help Hero *I'll make her come*. In addition, a statement is made to give more confidence and assurance that the promise will be carried out (*I warrant you*: +1). Moreover, Margaret exaggerates by saying that she will perform her promise without delay (*presently*: +1). This makes a total score of +3 only for positive politeness. Margaret is more polite than Hero.

In (7) Don Pedro's intention not to stay long in Messina is communicated with no apologetic tone. In fact, such an intention would be framed with polite strategies in a speech from the lower to the higher speaker, but this is not the case here since Don Pedro assumes more power than Claudio, who is only a count of Florence in Don Pedro's court. Claudio's response scores +1 for positive politeness because it expresses his offer to take Don Pedro to Arragon. With regard to negative politeness, the indirect request (*if you...*), expressed with the conditional force of the 'if-clause', scores +2 for deference, the deferential title *my lord* adds another point, which makes a total score of +4. Claudio is more polite than Don Pedro.

In (8), where Don John politely asks Don Pedro to speak to him before announcing to Don Pedro and Claudio that Hero is 'disloyal' (cf. 3, 2, 75-76), there are four instances of negative politeness, redressing the request. First, the request itself is indirect (*If your...*: +1); second, the use of the 'if-clause' provides the conditional force of the FTA (+1). Third, the use of the subjunctive *would*, which indicates uncertainty, adds another point. Fourth, there is what Brown and Levinson call "the use of point-of-view operations to *distance* S from H or from the particular FTA [...]. As the tense is switched from present into past, the speaker moves as if into the future, so he distances himself from the here and now. Hence, we get negatively polite FTAs with increasingly remote past tenses" (1987, 204). This strategy accounts for the use of the simple past instead of the present (*served*: +1), which brings the speech to a total score of +4. Don Pedro's response to Don John's request is a `verbless´ question, which scores no points for politeness. Don John is more polite than Don Pedro.

In (9) Hero's speech scores only +1 for positive politeness because of a positive politeness hedge *good*. Otherwise, the speech is spoken baldly on-record with the help of directives (*wake her, desire her*). Ursula responds with a promise (*I will...*), which scores +1 for positive politeness and another point for the deferential title *lady* (negative politeness), which makes a total score of +2. Ursula is more polite than Hero.

In (10) the FTA that Doggbery, the chief constable, has in mind is the trial of Conrade and Borachio, who agreed to help Don John destroy Hero's reputation, before Leonato, governor of Messina. As far as negative politeness is concerned, the speech scores +1 for minimisation *one word*, +3 for the deferential titles *sir*, used twice, and *your worship*, +1 for indicating scepticism through the modal verb *would*, and another point for the hedge *indeed*, making a total score of +6. Concerning positive politeness, the `collaborative´ plurals *our watch* and *we would*, which reflect Dogberry's pompous language, score +2. Altogether, negative politeness and positive politeness add up to a score of +8. Leonato's response, although it contains two commands *take* and *bring*, scores +1 for giving reasons *I am now in haste* (positive politeness) and another point for the `hedge´ *as it may appear unto you* (negative politeness). Dogberry's speech is more polite than Leonato's.

The first scene of *Measure for Measure* (11) opens with the Duke's calling Escalus only by his name, scoring no points for deference. This is no wonder since the Duke has more power than Escalus, who is only an ancient lord. In fact, it would not be impolite for a lord to be addressed only with his Christian name by a Duke, but it would be familiar by an equal and unthinkable by an inferior (cf. Reploge 1973, 173). Escalus' response scores +1 for negative politeness because it expresses deference through the honorific title *my lord*. Escalus is more polite than the Duke.

In (12) Angelo's surprise at his appointment leads him to protest and ask the Duke politely for a longer period of preparation. As far as negative politeness is concerned, the adorned title *good my lord* scores +2 for giving deference; *Let there be some more test of my metal* adds another point for deference, 'self-effacement' being a negative politeness strategy which includes statements where the speaker 'humbles and abases' himself. When this strategy is used Brown and Levinson indicate "that the addressee's [in this case the Duke's] rights to relative immunity from imposition are recognized - and moreover that [the speaker] is certainly not in a position to coerce [the hearer's] compliance in any way" (1987, 178).

To indicate that Angelo does not want to impinge on the Duke, he makes use of the passive (*some more test made of my metal, Be stamp'd upon it*: +2). According to Brown and Levinson (1987, 194), the passive, which promotes the underlying object and demotes the underlying subject, exists primarily as an impersonalising mechanism, that is, to avoid attributing the responsibility for an action to an agent. As to nominalisation, which occurs in *some more test* (+1), Brown and Levinson argue that "degrees of negative politeness (or at least formality) run hand in hand with nouniness" (1987, 207). Negative politeness thus reaches a score of +5. With respect to positive politeness, the speech scores +4 for exaggeration *so noble and so great*. Altogether, positive politeness and negative politeness make a total score of +9.

The Duke's response to Angelo's proposal is a severe rejection. He does not allow any questioning of his decision, however strange it may seem. To begin with, the Duke is 'rudely brusque' at the very beginning of his speech; his 'verbless imperative' *No more evasion* scores -1 for politeness. Being brusque, he asserts his power, denying the efficiency of Angelo's 'repair' strategies. Moreover, the delegation of power is confirmed by the 'regal plural' (*we have*, *we shall, our haste, our concernings, with us*). It is not until his use of subject-verb inversion that he speaks in the first person singular *do I leave you*. Furthermore, his directives (*take, do look*) score no points for politeness because they are baldly on-record. Finally, the Duke seems to have no positive evaluation of Angelo's positive face since he considers his proposal a matter of *needful value*. The Duke has more power than Angelo; accordingly, Angelo will be more polite than the Duke, and indeed he is.

In (13) Angelo, who is left in charge of affairs during the Duke's absence, is discussing the law with Escalus, an ancient lord. With regard to positive politeness, the speech scores +7: +5 for including the hearer in the activity (*we find, we stoop, we see, we do not, we tread upon*) and +2 for giving reasons (*Because we see it..., For I have had such*). As to negative politeness, the speech scores +2 for giving deference: +1 for humbling himself (*I have had such faults...*) and another point for the title *sir*. Escalus' response is less polite in terms of Brown and Levinson's politeness theory. The speech scores only +2 for negative politeness, +1 for giving deference *your wisdom*, whereas *Be it* (+1) is "not an action imperative but an agentless passive" (Brown and Gilman 1989, 160). In reality, (13) is to be considered neither strongly nor weakly contradictory to the theory because Angelo assumes more power than Escalus and behaves accordingly. It is true that Escalus is morally more indulgent than Angelo, but he is also 'weaker-willed', and his objections to Angelo's harshness in (2, 1, 4-16) do not have any effect but merely amount to indignant questions. Besides, Escalus' response, where he relapses into subservience, reflects the asymmetric power relation between the two. Angelo, as a deputy, is supposed to have more power than Escalus, and this is clear in the Duke's decision when conferring the office on Angelo:

Duke [...]. Old Escalus,
       Though first in question, is thy secondary.
       Take thy commission.
       (1, 1, 45-47)

Being merely Angelo's 'secondary', Escalus, surprisingly, asks Angelo to have a word with him as to his position in the government, where Angelo is head of state:

Escalus   I shall desire you, sir, to give me leave
       To have free speech with you; and it concerns me
       To look into the bottom of my place.
       A power I have, but of what strength and nature
       I am not yet instructed
       (1, 1, 76-80)

Escalus receives the answer in Angelo's speech in (13), where he is advised to mind his own business and stop meddling in Angelo's affairs. Accordingly, (13) is to be considered an instance confirming the theory.

In (14) Angelo's speech is much less polite than Elbow's; it scores only +1 (negative politeness) for the deferential title *sir*. Elbow, a simple constable, has arrested Pompey and Froth and attempts to have them imprisoned because Froth is accused of having done some 'unspeakable' wrong to Elbow's pregnant wife in the 'bawdy-house'. As to Pompey, he is employed by Mistress Overdone, a brothel-keeper, as a pander. Elbow's response to Angelo's speech is characterised by its deferential aspect. The indirect request (*If it please ...*) scores +2, the title *sir* +1, and the adorned title *your good honour* +2. By humbling himself, Elbow also expresses deference (*the poor Duke's constable, I do lean upon justice*: +2). Altogether, there is a score of +7 for negative politeness. Elbow is more polite than Angelo.

The contrast in (15) takes place in the same scene as (14), but now Escalus is left alone with Elbow and the two 'malefactors'. Pompey purposely disrupts the proceedings in order to unbalance Elbow's testimony; he even dares to argue the issue of sexual morality with the judge (Escalus) who has the power of life and death over him (cf. 2, 1, 205-09). As a result, Escalus addresses Pompey with a speech which, at first glance, seems to be polite. The scoring system allocates +1 for *Thank you* (positive politeness), and +1 for the deferential title *good Pompey*. Taking into consideration the mood established by what has preceded, i.e. Pompey's audacious speeches and the extreme incongruity of an ancient Lord saying *Thank you, good Pompey* to a 'bawd' in such a situation, one can be sure that the items scored are meant to be ironic, and it would be a mistake to score them as being polite. Moreover, the fact that the rest of Escalus' speech reveals the asymmetric power relation between the two supports the view that Escalus' apparent politeness is rather ironic. In fact, *I advice you*, uttered directly after the command *hark you*, threatens Pompey's face. Further, *I shall beat you* and *I shall have you whipt* express the same FTA, Escalus threatening to instigate sanctions against Pompey. Finally, Escalus emphasises his warnings by comparing himself to Caesar, who defeated Pompey the Great at Pharsalia in 48 BC (cf. Gibbons 1991, 107, n: 213-4).

Pompey's response scores +1 (positive politeness) because it expresses thankfulness for Escalus' advice *I thank your worship [...] counsel* and +1 (negative politeness) for the deferential title *your worship*. However, Pompey's soliloquy has to be taken into account. Only when alone, in the freedom of soliloquy, can he challenge Escalus and address him with no courtesy at all. His refusal to comply with Escalus' command is expressed through *but I shall follow it*, and his ridicule of Escalus can be seen in *wip me?*, which shows that Pompey really has a negative evaluation of Escalus' positive face. Pompey's soliloquy reveals his true attitude towards Escalus. His FTA is too risky to be openly expressed; it is an example of super-strategy (5) (cf. Fig. 1). The use of soliloquy thus enables the analyst to have access to the speaker's inner life. This is an instance of what Brown and Gilman refer to when they use drama as the corpus of a study of politeness. Pompey is more polite than Escalus.

In (16) Angelo rejects the Provost's plea to temper justice with mercy out of hand. In fact, the Provost's intervention in Angelo's decisions is a serious FTA because he imposes himself on Angelo's 'right to non-imposition'. His sharp directives (*Go to, Do, give up*) score no points for politeness, and they threaten the Provost's face, meaning that Angelo can easily manage without him: *you shall well be spared*. Angelo makes the Provost aware of the power he has over him, and the Provost responds accordingly. With respect to negative politeness, the Provost expresses deference through the titles (*your honour, sir*: +2) and the indirect request (*What shall be done, sir, with the groaning Juliet?*: +1); deference is also observed in the verb *crave*, with which the Provost humbles himself (+1). In addition, the speech scores another +1 for begging forgiveness *you honour's pardon*, +1 for the modal hedge *shall*, and +1 for the passive in *what shall be done?*, which brings it to a total score of +7 for negative politeness. Positive politeness, on the other hand, scores only +2: +1 for exaggeration *groaning Juliet* and +1 for giving reasons *She is very near her hour*, which produces a total score of +9. The Provost is more polite than Angelo.

In (17) Isabella is concerned with being polite because she comes to beg Angelo to spare her brother's life, who is arrested for impregnating Juliet, whom he regards as his wife. Only negative politeness occurs in her speech: the request to be heard *Please [...] hear me* scores +2 for deference; *you honour*, used twice, adds another +2. Deference is also observed in the adjective *woeful*, where she humbles herself +1. In addition, the speech scores +2, +1 for minimisation *but you honour* and +1 for nominalisation *woeful suitor*, which produces a total score of +7. Angelo's response scores only +1 (negative politeness) for the `adverbial hedge' *well*. Isabella is more polite than Angelo.

In (18) Pompey, arrested as a `bawd', politely asks Lucio to pay a sum of money for him and thus secure his freedom. The indirect request (*I hope...*) scores +1 for giving deference; the deferential titles (*sir*: +1, *your good worship*: +2) add another three points for deference. In addition, the `polite pessimism' which is expressed in *I hope*, brings the speech to a total score of +5 just for negative politeness. In his response, Lucio is quite indifferent to Pompey's imprisonment; he refuses to go bail for him, however long or hard his imprisonment will be. *Adieu, trusty Pompey* seems to score +2 for politeness, but Lucio's intentions *I will pay, Pompey, to increase your bondage* prove that it would be a mistake to think he cares to be polite. Therefore, the two points should perhaps be taken off. Pompey is more polite than Lucio.

In (19) Abhorson, a public executioner, is impolite to Pompey, who is offered the choice of becoming deputy executioner or suffering imprisonment for the rest of his life (cf. 4, 2, 5-11). The two commands (*come on, follow*) score no points for politeness but reflect an asymmetric power relation since Abhorson addresses Pompey with simple imperatives appropriate for speaking to an inferior. Furthermore, Abhorson has no positive evaluation of Pompey's face because identifying Pompey in terms of his past occupation as a 'bawd' means that he is not willing to accept him as a deputy executioner, i.e. Abhorson is proud of his work and unwilling to teach it to Pompey. However, under the influence of the Provost (cf. 4, 2, 23), he promises to instruct him, his promise *I will instruct thee* scoring +1 for positive politeness. Pompey's response reflects his ambition to learn what Abhorson calls 'our mystery' (cf. 4, 2, 22). With regard to negative politeness, the deferential title *sir*, used twice, scores +2, and the indirect request (*if you have...*), accessed with the force of the 'if-clause', adds two points for deference. Further deference is observed in *I do desire to learn*, in which Pompey humbles his capacities (+1). In addition, the expression of scepticism through *I hope* scores +1 and the hedge *truly* adds another point, bringing the score to +7 for negative politeness. As to positive politeness, the speech scores +1 because it expresses admiration for Abhorson's face *your kindness*, and another two points for asserting 'reciprocity' (*for your own turn* [...] *yare, I owe you a good turn*). Altogether, negative politeness and positive politeness add to a score of +9 in Pompey's response to Abhorson. Pompey is more polite than Abhorsen.

In (20) Friar Peter's role is to bring Isabella and Mariana where they can petition the Duke, whose plan is to destroy Angelo through Isabella's and Mariana's denunciations. The Friar's testimony that Angelo is innocent shows that he is working 'covertly' against Isabella. He starts his speech with wishing the Duke what the Duke wishes for himself (*Blessed be...*); the salutation scores +1 for positive politeness since the Friar asks God's favour for the Duke and so the Duke's positive face is satisfied. With respect to negative politeness, the adorned title *your royal grace* scores +2 and the deferential title *my lord* adds another point. By referring to the Duke's *ear* instead of the Duke himself, the Friar dissociates the Duke from criticism (+1), which results in a total score of +4 for negative politeness. Altogether, positive politeness and negative politeness reach a score of +5. The Duke's response scores no points for politeness; it only reflects power relations through the 'royal plural' *we*. Friar Peter is more polite than the Duke.

In (21) Lucio, a 'fantastic', is concerned about being polite; his speech scores +1 for negative politeness because it expresses deference through the deferential title *my lord*. In being polite, Lucio is trying to win over Escalus so as to get 'Friar Lodowick' punished, whom he falsely accuses of slandering the Duke (Lucio does not know that 'Friar Lodowick' and the Duke are one and the same person). Escalus' speech, on the other hand, contains a command which is meant to prevent Lucio from speaking to 'Friar Lodowick' before he is granted permission to do so. Besides, it might also be argued that he is expected to listen without interruption, and patiently takes his turn when Escalus is speaking (cf. dyad (45), for instance, where Lucio is taught by the Duke to behave himself and stop interrupting him). Moreover, the use of the 'regal plural' in *till we call upon you* emphasises the asymmetric power relation between Escalus and Lucio. Escalus is less polite than Lucio.

In (22) Mariana, Angelo's cast-off fiancée, politely rejects the Duke's offer to buy her 'a better husband' by confiscating Angelo's property (cf. 5, 1, 411-18). She is pleading for Angelo's life and tries to save him from the 'gallows' despite all his crimes and lies to her. Her speech, although short, is considerably polite. As far as negative politeness is concerned, the adorned title *my dear Lord* scores +2 for deference. By insisting on keeping Angelo as a husband, Mariana shows that she is content with him and does not need a 'better husband'. In doing so, she is actually abasing herself (+1). Positive politeness, on the other hand, scores only +1 for the interjection *O*, which brings the speech to a total score of +4. The regal response of the Duke scores no points for politeness. The adverb *never*, which is used as an emphatic substitute for the negation 'not', adds more power to the Duke's use of the imperative *Never crave him*. Moreover, the Duke's refusal to negotiate can be seen in his use of the 'royal plural' *we* and in the adjective *definitive*, which emphasise that his decision is to be looked upon as final, excluding any possibility of change. Mariana is more polite than the Duke.

In (23) Isabella, in an intense moment, kneels down to plead for the man who is supposed to have killed her brother because Marina, Angelo's cast-off fiancée, urges her to do so (cf. 5, 1, 429-35). Although she is polite, her plea cuts no ice at all with the Duke. With regard to negative politeness, if her kneeling down is to be understood as a 'non-verbal' marker of politeness, then she is, of course, humbling herself and showing deference (+1). Further deference occurs in the adorned title (*bounteous sir*: +2) and in the indirect request (*if it please...*: +2). The utterances *I partly think* (+1), *but justice* (+1), *but as an intent* (+1), *but merely* (+2) work together to minimise the imposition of Isabella's FTA (+5). With regard to the adverb 'partly', Gibbons argues "[i]t is significant that Isabella includes the modifying adverb 'partly' suggesting perhaps reluctance to change her view, or the dawning - but not yet full - realisation of the idea that she unwittingly tempted Angelo. Her phrasing nevertheless implies her passivity in interviews with Angelo" (1991, 189, n: 438-40). The speech also scores +1 for the passive *must be buried*, and +1 for nominalisation *his bad intent*, which brings it to +12. As far as positive politeness is concerned, the speech scores +1 for exaggeration *most*, and +1 for giving reasons *In that he did the thing for which he died*, which makes a total score of +14.

The Duke's response to Isabella is a severe rejection of her plea. The harsh connotation of the word *unprofitable* seems in itself cruel. The rejection is further stressed by the command *Stand up* and the emphatic *I say*, by means of which the effectiveness of Isabella's kneeling down is denied and the Duke's power is asserted. The asymmetric power relation is reflected in the two speeches because Isabella is more polite than the Duke.

In (24) the Duke manifests his power by deciding, not in earnest, to dismiss the provost from office since he merely had a 'private message' instead of an official written order for the execution of Claudio (cf. 5, 1, 450-53). The Duke's decision is emphasised by his command *Give up your keys*. The Provost's response is apologetic. With respect to negative politeness, his speech scores +2 for the deferential adorned title *noble Lord*, +1 for humbling himself by admitting his responsibility *it was a fault*, +1 for begging forgiveness *Pardon me*, +1 for expressing regret *Yet did me repent*, and +3 for nominalisation (*it was a fault, more advice, For testimony*), which makes a total score of +8 for negative politeness. As to positive politeness, the speech scores only +2 for giving reasons *but know it not, For testimony whereof* [...] *I have reserved alive*, which brings it to a total score of +10. The Provost is more polite than the Duke.

In (25) when the Duke is no longer disguised and everything is revealed, Lucio begs the Duke not to marry him to a prostitute who has born his child. Negative politeness shows up massively to express deference: the indirect request (*I beseech...*) scores +2, *your highness*, used twice, adds another +2, the adorned title *good my lord* +2 as well. Giving reasons *Your highness said even now I made you a duk* scores +1 for positive politeness, which makes a total score of +7. The Duke's response to Lucio's request scores no points for politeness; it is, in fact, a revengeful act because Lucio has shamelessly slandered the Duke to the Friar, not realising that they are one and the same person. The asymmetry power relation between the two is observed when he swears by his honour that his command must be carried out *Upon mine honour, thou shall marry her*. Moreover, such a relation is reflected in his command *Take him to prison* and in the use of the 'royal plural' *our pleasure herein executed*. The Duke is less polite than Lucio.

In the Induction to *The Taming of the Shrew* (26) the lord, who is returning from hunting, starts his speech by making some 'judicious' remarks about his dogs, then changes the course of the conversation by using the conjunction 'but', followed by two imperatives *sup* and *look on*. Nevertheless, his speech scores +1 for giving reasons for his FTA *Tomorrow I intend to hunt again*. The First Huntsman's response scores +1 for positive politeness because he promises to do the FTA imposed on him. As to negative politeness, the deferential title *my lord* adds another point, which brings the speech to total score of +2. The lord is less polite than the First Huntsman.

In (27) the lord is actually obeyed by everybody; he addresses his servant with the 'contemptuous' form of address *sirrah*, which scores -1 for deference, and baldly on-record sends his servant to carry out his order *go* and *see*. He also shows little concern about being polite after the return of his servant: he is too impatient and only wants to satisfy his curiosity. In fact, his powerful style *how now? who is it?* shows that he is in a relation of dominance over his servant. The servant's powerless speech, on the other hand, scores +2 because it expresses deference through the deferential titles *you honour* and *your lordship*. Further deference is conveyed in the indirect request (*An't please...*:+2). Moreover, the 'old use' of the 'if-clause' *An't*, which functions as a hedge, adds another point, making a total score of +5 for negative politeness. The speech of the lower (the servant) to the higher (the lord) is more polite.

In (28) the lord's FTA is done indirectly since it questions the hearer's intention and thus scores +1 for deference (negative politeness). The player's response is obviously more deferential. The indirect request (*So please...*) scores +2 for deference, and the deferential title *you honour* +1. Further deference is expressed when the player considers his activity as a *duty*. In doing so, he humbles himself and those in whose name he speaks. Another point is thus added, which bring the speech to a total score of +4 for negative politeness alone. The player is more polite than the lord.

Both speeches in (29) are polite, but Lucentio has more power than his servant, Tranio, and so politeness theory predicts that Tranio will be more polite than Lucentio, as indeed he is. To start with, Lucentio addresses Tranio only with his name (Line 17) and uses a simple imperative *tell me*. However, positive politeness shows up many times: exaggeration (*well, in all*: +2), showing admiration (*approved, good company, trusty servant*: +3), giving reasons (*for I have left*: +1), and claiming 'common ground' (*let us breathe*: +1), for a total score of +7.

Tranio's response provides a variety of positive politeness strategies, which include giving reasons (*As Ovid be an outcast quite abjured, Music and poesy use to quicken you*: +2), using inclusive forms (*let, we*: +2), exaggerating sympathy (*I am in all affected*: +1), and showing admiration (*Glad that you thus continue your resolve*: +1), which amounts to a total score of +6 for positive politeness. As to negative politeness, Tranio starts by apologising to his master before telling his mind (*Mi perdonto*: +1). The adorned deferential titles *gentle master* and *good master* score +4, whereas the unadorned title *sir* only +1. Further deference is present in the indirect request *pray you* (+1). Moreover, the speech scores +1 for nominalisation *your resolve*, +1 for minimisation *Only*, and +1 for the 'quantity hedge' *in brief*, which brings the speech to a total score of +10. Altogether, positive politeness and negative politeness add up to a score of +17, which makes the speech one of the politest in the play. Tranio is more polite than Lucentio.

In (30) Petruchio, a gentleman of Verona, starts his speech by explaining where he is and why to his servant, Grumio, who is addressed with the 'contemptuous form of address' *sirrah*, which scores -1 for deference. Moreover, Petruchio's power reveals itself in the command *knock*, which is given stress by the emphatic *I say*. In Grumio's response, there is a misunderstanding on the object of the verb 'knock', Petruchio wants Grumio to 'knock' at Hortentio's door, but Grumio wrongly assumes a (missing) accusative, meaning 'hit' (cf. Thompson 1984, 69, n: 8). However, the deferential titles *sir* and *your worship* score +2 for negative politeness. Grumio is more polite than Petruchio.

In (31) Petruchio is extravagantly impolite; he is insulting and threatening the tailor, and these FTAs are directed at the hearer's positive face. Furthermore, they are made more threatening by the use of the 'verbless imperative' (*Away*: -1) and the 'isolated thou' in *thou winter-cricket thou* (-1). The tailor is treated abominably; Thompson even argues that "[t]he tailor's trade, having an appearance of effeminacy has always been, among the ragged English, liable to sarcasms and contempt" (ibid., 129, n: 106-13). However, in spite of this apparent impoliteness, it should be born in mind that the speech, in which Petruchio, on purpose, throws away beautiful clothes made for Katharina, belongs to his taming plan (cf. 4, 3, 18-20, for instance, where Katharina is even denied food). Petruchio is not in a state of rage, his impoliteness is not to be taken seriously. The tailor's response scores +1 because it expresses deference *your worship*, +2 for the passive *your worship is deceived* and *the gown is made*, and +1 for the hedge *just*, which makes a total score of +4 for negative politeness. Positive politeness, on the other hand, scores only +1 for giving reasons *Grumio gave order how it should be done*, which brings the speech to a total score of +5. The tailor is more polite than Petruchio.

The speech in (32), in which Vincentio addresses Biondello, Lucentio's servant, is not polite; it is an FTA to Biondello's positive face. In fact, Biondello is surprised to see his 'old master', Vincentio, in Verona at the same time the pedant plays the role of Vincentio, Lucentio's father, and is useful in arranging Lucentio's marriage to Bianca. Being frightened 'We are undone [ruined]' (cf. 5, 1, 35), he in vain tries to avoid Vincentio. The command *come hither* and the incivility expressed in the swearword *crack-hemp* clearly establish an asymmetric power relation. Biondello's response, on the other hand, scores +1 because it expresses uncertainty about the success of his FTA *I hope*. The impact of the FTA is also hedged by the modal verb *may* (+1); in addition, the use of the deferential title *sir* brings the speech to a total score of +3 for negative politeness. Biondello, who is only a servant, is more polite than Vincentio, who is a rich old citizen of Pisa.

In *Twelfth Night* (33) Curio, Orsino's courtier, addresses Orsino, the Duke, with a speech which scores +1 for its indirectness and another point for the deferential title *my lord*, which gives a total score of +2 for negative politeness. The Duke's response to Curio's question reflects the asymmetry power relation existing between the two. He is not concerned about framing his answer with polite markers and prefers the bald on-record alternative.

The notable contrast in the two speeches in (34) lies in the efficiency of the first and the politeness of the second. Olivia, who is a countess, satisfies Grice's Maxims of Conversation in that she communicates only what is necessary. The order *speak to me* and the question *your will* are not mitigated by any polite markers and thus score no points for politeness. Viola, a shipwrecked girl who is pretending to be a man on his way to deliver a love message from Orsino, responds with a speech that says more than is necessary and so sacrifices `efficiency´ in order to accomplish politeness. Positive politeness is used numerous times, including complimenting (*beauty, beauties*: +2), giving reasons (*for I never saw her, for besides it is excellently well penned, I have taken great pains to con it, I am very compatible*: +4), exaggerating (*even to the least sinister usage*: +1) and hedging the admiration for Olivia through the items (*most, radiant, exquisite, unmatchable, good*: +5). With regard to mitigating admiration, Brown and Levinson argue that "one positive politeness output (strategy 2) leads S to exaggerate [...]. For this reason, one characteristic device in positive politeness is to hedge these extremes, so as to make one´s opinion safely vague. Normally hedges are a feature of negative politeness [...] but some hedges can have this positive function as well" (1987, 116). Positive politeness thus reaches a score of +12.

As to negative politeness, the indirect request *I pray* scores +1 for deference, and the use of the subjunctive *would*, functioning as a hedge, adds another point, which makes a total score of +2. Altogether, positive politeness and negative politeness reach a total score of +14. Viola is more polite than Olivia.

Malvolio´s speech in (35) is a good example to illustrate Brown and Levinson´s notion of deference: "There are two sides to the coin in the realization of deference: one in which S humbles and abases himself, and another where S raises H [...]. In both cases what is conveyed is that H is of a higher social status than S" (1987, 178). *At your service* is an instance where Malvolio, Olivia´s steward, humbles himself; using *madam*, he raises her by addressing her with the deferential title, corresponding to a woman of high status. The two instances score +2 for negative politeness. Olivia calls for Malvolio to come directly after her soliloquy (cf. 1, 5, 244-54), in which her fascination for Cesario/Viola is revealed. Her desire to remain in contact with him can be seen in her ring trick: Olivia tells Malvolio that Cesario left a ring behind, which is not true, but she apologises for the trick, cf. dyad (42). Malvolio is sent to catch up with Cesario and give him the ring back. In such a state of emergency she addresses her steward only with his name. In addition, she makes an extensive use of directives which are baldly on-record (*run, desire, hold him up, hie thee*). Malvolio is more polite than Olivia.

In (36) the Clown takes Sebastian for his sister, Viola. His FTA is performed indirectly since it is framed in the form of an interrogative, thus scoring +1 for deference (negative politeness). Sebastian, who does not know that he is mistaken for Cesario/Viola, responds by using the command *go to*, which is emphasised by the use of the same imperative a second time, as he thinks that the Clown is making fun of him. Moreover, by insulting the Clown *thou art a foolish fellow*, Sebastian shows that he has a negative evaluation of the Clown's positive face, while his powerful dismissal of the Clown *Let me be clear of thee* sounds like an order to an inferior servant. The Clown is more polite than Sebastian.

Orsino's speech in (37) scores no points for politeness. Being a Duke, he dares to insult Antonio, who is arrested as an enemy of the state. The affronts (*Notable pirate, thief, foolish boldness*) are threats to the hearer's positive face (cf. Brown/Levinson 1987, 66). In Antonio's response, negative politeness occurs many times. The adorned deferential title *noble sir* scores +2; the request (*Be pleased...*: +1) "is not an action imperative but an `agentless passive´ which has no presumption in it" (Brown and Levinson 1989, 160). Moreover, Antonio's confession that he is Orsino's enemy *I confess* is an instance of `self-effacement´, where Antonio humbles himself; this strategy adds another point for deference. Furthermore, impersonalisation strategy is evident in (*Antonio never yet...*); here Antonio distances himself as an individual from the accusation brought against him by avoiding the pronoun *I* (+1) (cf. Brown/Levinson 1987, 204). Negative politeness also works by dissociation. In *A witchcraft drew me here* Antonio dissociates himself from having intentionally come to Illyria, thereby indicating that his presence is forced by external circumstances. In doing so, his reluctance to impinge on the Duke becomes more justified (+1). Furthermore, nominalisation is also at work (*All his in dedication*: +1), which brings the speech to a total score of +7 only for negative politeness. Positive politeness, on the other hand, scores only +1 for giving reasons *For his sake did I expose myself* [...] *apprehended*, which makes a total score of +8. Antonio is more polite than the Duke.

With respect to the variable power (P), positive politeness and negative politeness are interwoven, and it is important to distinguish between them in the scoring because a person with less power would prefer to use negative politeness strategies whereas a person with more power would tend to use positive ones. As already mentioned (cf. 2.2.2), the essence of negative politeness is deference; this is why a person with less power would normally feel obliged to use negative politeness. On the other hand, the nature of positive politeness is solidarity: a person with more power would normally choose positive politeness. Table 7 below shows that the 37 dyads analysed so far confirm Brown and Levinson's theory in that the speeches of the person with less power score considerably more politeness strategies than the ones of the person with more power (199 versus 27). Table 7 below also shows that Brown and Levinson's model predicts that in an asymmetrical relationship, a subordinate addressing a superior would rationally choose strategies of negative politeness because risk of 'face loss' to a superior is relatively serious (150 for negative politeness as against 49 for positive politeness), while a superior addressing a subordinate would use positive politeness because risk of `face loss´ to a subordinate is relatively unimportant (24 for positive politeness as against three for negative politeness).

Outcomes of power congruent with the theory	The person with less power			The person with more power		
	Negative politeness	Positive politeness	Total	Negative politeness	Positive politeness	Total
1	4	0	4	0	2	2
2	3	0	3	0	0	0
3	1	1	2	0	0	0
4	8	0	8	1	0	1
5	1	2	3	0	0	0
6	0	3	3	0	1	1
7	3	1	4	0	0	0
8	4	0	4	0	0	0
9	1	1	2	0	1	1
10	6	2	8	1	1	2
11	1	0	1	0	0	0
12	5	4	9	-1	0	-1
13	2	0	2	2	7	9
14	7	0	7	1	0	1
15	1	1	2	1	1	2
16	7	2	9	0	0	0
17	7	0	7	1	0	1
18	5	0	5	0	2	2
19	7	3	10	0	1	1
20	4	1	5	0	0	0
21	1	0	1	0	0	0
22	3	1	4	0	0	0
23	12	2	14	0	0	0
24	8	2	10	0	0	0
25	6	1	7	0	0	0
26	1	1	2	0	1	1
27	5	0	5	-1	0	-1
28	4	0	4	1	0	1
29	10	7	17	0	7	7
30	2	0	2	-1	0	-1
31	4	1	5	-2	0	-2
32	3	0	3	0	0	0
33	2	0	2	0	0	0
34	2	12	14	0	0	0
35	2	0	2	0	0	0
36	1	0	1	0	0	0
37	7	1	8	0	0	0
Total	150	49	199	3	24	27

Table 7. Positive and negative politeness strategies used in power (P) contrasts

4. 1. 2 Contrasts contradicting the theory

4. 1. 2. 1 Strongly contradictory contrasts

In *Much Ado about Nothing* (38) Hero, the daughter of the Governor of Messina, addresses her maid, Margaret, with a courteous speech. The deferential indirect request *pray thee* scores +1 for negative politeness, and the diminutive *Meg* adorned with the positive politeness hedge *good* adds two points for positive politeness, making a total score of +3. Margaret, in her response and in the whole scene "is nervous and rapid and full of elision [...] she was dressed in Hero's clothes and entertaining Borachio" (Mares 1988, 105, n: 7), thus unwittingly assisting the plot to discredit Hero before her wedding. Her nervousness and embarrassment may, therefore, account for her impoliteness to Hero. Her disagreement with Hero is a threat to Hero's positive face because her choice of clothes is considered to be wrong and thus disapproved. Hero stands higher than her servant, and so far as power considerations go, should feel no compulsion to be polite. What happens in (38) is quite the opposite. Hero is being polite, cf. dyad (68), in which Margaret's speech causes Hero to be suddenly impolite to her.

In *Measure for Measure* Isabella's speech in (39) is a challenge to Angelo and thus a threat to his positive face since she thinks he is unreasonable in his verdict to execute her brother, Claudio. Her bald on-record strategy can be observed in the use of the directives (*Go to, Knock, ask, Let it*), which unmask Angelo. First, although Isabella has not yet heard of Mariana, Angelo's cast-off fiancée, her speech awakens his guilt for his past treatment of Mariana *Go to your bosom* [...] *brother's life*; second, Isabella's speech motivates Angelo to confess his `guilty desire´ to have sexual intercourse in his soliloquy at the start of his response (cf. Gibbons 1984, 32). Angelo does not react with utterances like

'Away with her' or 'Let me be clear of thee', as one may expect. On the contrary, he bids her farewell *fare you well*, which scores +1 for positive politeness. Angelo, although a lord, is being more polite than Isabella, who is only a nun.

In (40) Pompey, now a deputy executioner, is sent to fetch Barnardine, a 'dissolute' prisoner, for execution so that his head can be disguised as Claudio's and sent to Angelo. The scoring system allocates +1 for each deferential *sir* and another point for the use of the 'in-group identity' term *your friends* (positive politeness), which gives a total score of +3. Barnardine's response, although it scores +1 for giving reasons *I am sleepy*, is a threat to Pompey's positive face because it contains an insult *you rogue* and the 'verbless imperative' *away*, which is used twice (-2). It is almost dawn and Barnardine is still a little under the effect of alcohol, which may account for his impoliteness. According to Brown and Gilman (1989, 189-90), drunkenness is overlooked in the scoring. However, Barnardine cannot be compared to the drunken Cassio's incivility in *Othello* (cf. 3.2.2).

The interesting aspect about the contrast in (40) is, however, Pompey's ironic language. To score his *sirs* as deferential and *your friend* as an instance of positive politeness would therefore be a mistake. The following quotation taken from Kendall (1981, 245-46) can clarify this point:

> There are major analytic advantages to viewing humans as actors who create and interpret meanings rather than 'subjects' who respond to features. One of the most notable is that the former position renders intelligible all the highly creative plays on order and regularity that the latter position cannot touch. It allows one to account for ironic forms of address, whether they be humorous or sarcastic [...]. To understand that an instance of address is humorous, a person has to understand the conventional meaning of the form to be sure; but the person must also understand that the speaker intends to use the form non-seriously (Kendall 1981, 245-46).

Accordingly, Pompey knows that Barnardine can recognise sarcastic intonation, i.e. the falseness of Pompey's polite statement is made clear by a 'contradictory tone of the utterance' (cf. Leech 1984, 142-43). Barnardine can understand that the use of *your friends* does not imply 'solidarity'. Likewise, he knows that the deferential *sirs* carry a more heavily ironic message because a deputy executioner does not address people who are sentenced to death with such terms. He also knows that a powerful person accords himself or herself the right to impose his or her power prerogative on persons with less power, i.e. to address them baldly on-record. In fact, (40) is only an apparently contradictory contrast because Pompey is not really more polite than Barnardine. However, it is an interesting dyad because of its important implications for politeness theory, i.e. Pompey's use of irony.

In *The Taming of the Shrew* Katharina (41) is in the course of being tamed by Petruchio's behaviour, which is more outrageous and extravagant than her shrewdness. For instance, she is even denied food by Petruchio's servant, Grumio. As a result she contents herself with whatever she is offered to eat, thereby implicitly abasing herself (negative politeness: +1); this is clearly observed in her exaggeration (*passing good*: +2) (positive politeness). In addition, there is an indirect request *I prithee*, which adds another point for giving deference (negative politeness), making a total score of +3. Grumio's response proves that he is acting in collaboration with Petruchio as Katharina receives no food. On the contrary, Grumio decides to go on mocking her and suggests another sort of food. His ridicule of Katharina shows that he has no positive evaluation of her positive face. Katharina is more polite than Grumio.

In *Twelfth Night* Olivia, thinking that Viola is a man, falls in love with her. Her change of attitude towards Cesario/Viola is reflected in her linguistic behaviour. In (42) she is extremely polite, which is not the case in Olivia's earlier speeches to her, cf. dyad (34). Her speech reveals a marked preference for negative politeness: the three indirect requests (*Give me leave*: +2, *beseech you*: +2, *what might you think?*: +1) score +5 for deference. Further deference is expressed by her self-abasement (*so did I abuse myself, shameful cunning*, and *a cypress, not a bosom, hideth my heart*: +3). In addition to giving deference, she begs forgiveness (*I fear me*: +1). Nominalisation is also at work (*hard construction, shameful cunning, your receiving*: +3). Moreover, the 'hypothetical' hedge *might* in the indirect request, cited above, indicates scepticism (+1), which brings the speech to a total score of +13 for negative politeness alone. Cesario/Olivia's response, on the other hand, scores only +1 for positive politeness 'I pity you'. The speech from the higher to the lower is the more polite.

In (43) Sir Toby, who permanently mocks Malvolio in the play, addresses Malvolio with *man*, a familiar form of address. Malvolio knows that Sir Toby, his social superior, is being unpleasant to him, and that the use of positive politeness *man* is insincere and ironic. However, this insincerity does not give Malvolio sufficient grounds for being impolite. First, he imposes on Sir Toby by asking him twice to *go off*; second, he treats Sir Toby as if he were a worthless person: *I discard you*. Third, Malvolio claims the right to non-imposition *let me enjoy my private*. All these prerogatives belong to a duke, not to a steward like Malvolio. His powerful speech does not fit his social rank. Malvolio is less polite than Sir Toby.

4. 1. 2. 2 Weakly contradictory contrasts

In *Much Ado about Nothing* (44) Don Pedro, who is a duke, is more polite than Balthasar, the musician in the service of the Duke. As far as negative politeness is concerned, the indirect request *I pray thee* scores +1 for giving deference, and the modal hedge *would* adds another point. As to positive politeness, the speech scores +1 for giving reasons (*for tomorrow...*), producing a total score of +3. Balthasar's response scores +1 for offering the *best* he could (positive politeness) and another point for the deferential title *my lord* (negative politeness), which makes a total score of +2. The dyad is weakly contradictory to the theory because Don Pedro and Balthasar speak with a similar politeness.

The speech in (45) takes place during the trial scene in *Measure for Measure* when the Duke is no longer disguised. Being disturbed by Lucio's successive interruptions, the Duke politely attempts to silence him. The speech scores +1 for indicating uncertainty *I wish*, and +2 for the indirect requests *pray you* and *pray heaven,* which gives a total score of +3. Lucio is asked to stop interrupting the Duke because interruptions are FTAs, indicating indifference to the hearer's positive face (cf. Brown/Levinson 1987, 67). In his response, Lucio seems to have learnt the lesson since he promises to behave himself (*I warrant*: +1) (positive politeness). In addition, there is a deferential title *you honour*, which adds another point (negative politeness), which makes a total score of +2. If Brown and Gilman's scoring system is followed, it is true that the Duke's speech is more polite than Lucio's, but it would be a mistake to treat (45) as strongly contradictory to the theory because both participants use polite markers in an asymmetric power relation. Moreover, even Brown and Gilman (1989, 193) admit that the scoring system is not one hundred percent objective.

In *Twelfth Night* (46) Duke Orsino is not concerned about being polite when addressing the Clown; this is perfectly in agreement with politeness theory because, as far as power relations are concerned, Orsino stands higher than the Clown. It is true that the Clown's response scores +1 for the deferential title *sir*, but he is expected to be more polite. However, he does not employ honorific titles proper for a duke, such as `my lord´, `your worship´, `your grace´, etc. The aim of the directive *Put your grace in your pocket* is to tell Orsino to forget being a duke (cf. Donno 1985, 134, n: 25): a serious FTA to Orsino's positive face. So far one may argue that the two matched speeches yield a result that is weakly contradictory to the theory. However, the Clown's audacious speech may be attributed to Orsino's weak personality. His rank is, in fact, not clear; he is known to be a duke and named so in speech headings, but quite often he is just called `count´ (cf. Donno 1985, 16). Following Turner (1975), Donno argues that Shakespeare made Orsino's character less of a figure of authority (Ibid.). A piece of evidence which lends support to this argument is the fact that Olivia, only a countess, is given far more speeches (117) than Orsino (58). Hence, the poor number of the power (P) contrasts in *Twelfth Night*: only (4).

4. 2 Extremity

To test the effect of "the extremity of the FTA, a given speaker must make two-face-threatening speeches, of clearly unequal extremity, to a given hearer" (Brown and Gilman 1989, 196). Table 8 below shows that the distribution of the contrasts of extremity (R) in the four plays is not strikingly different, ranging from 4 to 6. *Much Ado about Nothing* scores slightly higher than *Twelfth Night* (6 versus 4), while *Measure for Measure* and *The Taming of the Shrew* are in between, each scoring five contrasts. There are 19 such contrasts in the plays, and all of them are congruent with the theory. The effect of the variable rank is thus consistently in agreement with Brown and Levinson's theory. In what follows, each minimal pair will be considered in turn.

Play	Congruent with theory[a]	Weakly contradictory to theory[b]	Strongly contradictory to theory[c]	Total
Much Ado about Nothing	6	0	0	6
Measure for Measure	5	0	0	5
The Taming of the Shrew	5	0	0	5
Twelfth Night	4	0	0	4
Total	20	0	0	20

Table 8. Contrasts of extremity alone
   [a] The more extreme face threat is more politely expressed
   [b] Two face threats, differing in extremity, are expressed with equal politeness
   [c] The more extreme face threat is less politely expressed

In *Much Ado about Nothing* Claudio (47), talking to Don Pedro, clearly makes two speeches of unequal extremity. The second one is moderately polite: the honorific title *my Lord* scores +1 for negative politeness (give deference). His first speech is, however, strikingly more polite. The indirect request (*My liege...*) scores +2; the honorific title *your highness* +1; the modal *may*, which functions as a mitigating marker, adds another point. The total politeness score is thus +4. Claudio's behaviour in his second speech suggests that he has in mind an extreme request.

The conversation continues:

Claudio: Hath Leonato any son, my Lord? (2, 3, 220)

This reveals the purpose of the request: Claudio wants to know whether Hero is Leonato's only heir. From the start he is a prudent lover and investigates Hero's prospects; Prouty argues from a study of Elizabethan marriage customs that "Claudio is a careful suitor with an interest in finances" (1950, 43). Being aware of the seriousness of his FTA, Claudio makes his first speech more polite and communicates his real message to Don Pedro without being `overtly obtrusive´ on Don Pedro's `freedom of action´.

(48) shows a similar contrast. Leonato's first speech, a direct offer to Claudio, scores only +1 for the deferential title *Count* (negative politeness).

However, in his second speech Leonato is more polite although he is still addressing the same person. *My dear son* scores +1 for "positive politeness strategy (4): Use in-group identity terms" (Brown and Gilman 1989, 184). In addition, the adjective *dear* conveys more affection and scores another point for positive politeness. *A just seven-night* and *a time too brief* minimise the imposition (+2). Leonato thus indicates that the intrinsic seriousness of the imposition is not great. He also gives reasons for his FTA, i.e. *to have all things answer my mind*, which brings the speech to a total score of +5. The massive addition of redress in the second speech reflects the extremity (R) of Leonato´s request: to postpone the marriage. Clearly enough, the more extreme FTA is more polite.

In (49) Don John puts his plan to destroy Hero´s marriage ceremony into practice. In his first speech, he is polite. The request itself is indirect (*If it please you...*) and scores +2 for negative politeness. *Count Claudio* gives deference (+1), and the modal *may* is a hedge (+1 for negative politenes). Giving reasons *for what I speak of concerns him* scores +1 for positive politeness, which brings the total politeness score to +5. Having richly redressed his request, Don John moves on to express his more serious FTA: to announce to Claudio and Don Pedro that `the lady is disloyal´.

DON JOHN   I came hither to tell you; and, circumstances shortened [leaving out
the details] for she has been too long a talking of, the lady is
disloyal.
(3, 2, 75-6)

In his second speech Don John is not concerned about being polite because of the degree of the ranked extremity of his FTA, which is not as serious as the first one. *Let us go* is an indirect imperative and scores +1 for positive politeness (Include the hearer in the activity). Don John is only suggesting to Don

Pedro and Claudio that they should leave after he has succeeded in breaking up Hero's wedding. The two FTAs in (49) are of unequal extremity, and this accounts for the different 'investment' of politeness.

In (50) the first speech is less polite than the second. Dogberry begins by asserting his power with *Ha, ah, ha!*, which is "[a] crow of triumph, rather than a laugh" (Marres 1988, 70, n: 70). Moreover, he does not care to soften his directives (*call up, keep, come*). The honorific title *masters* gives deference (+1 for negative politeness). The salutation *good night* scores +1 for positive politeness, and *neighbour* is positive politeness again (+1). The total score is thus +3. Dogberry is addressing his inferiors with routine courtesy, demanding that they resort to him in case of 'weight chances'. In his second speech Dogberry is extravagantly polite. In framing his request he begins by minimising his FTA *one word*, which scores +1 for negative politeness. *Honest neighbours* score +2 for positive politeness (use in-group identity terms), and +1 for the indirect request *I pray you*. Giving reasons for his FTA *for the wedding being there tomorrow* scores another +1 for positive politeness, and *Adieu* is positive politeness as well (+1). To conclude his speech, Dogberry emphasises the indirectness of his request with *I beseech you*, which scores another +2 for negative politeness. The total score is +9, which makes this speech one of the politest in the play. The two speeches are clearly of unequal extremity (R), and this is reflected in the number of politeness strategies used to mitigate his FTA: his watchmen should 'watch about Leonato's door'. Otherwise, if something unpleasant happens, Dogberry will be the object of criticism for laxity by his superior, Leonato.

Addressing Leonato this time, Dogberry's first speech in (51) does not lack politeness. After the initial expression of deference *your worship*, which scores +1 for negative politeness, Dogberry expresses positive politeness, first through *I praise God for you*, which scores another +1, and, second, through exaggeration (*most thankful and reverend*: +3). However, Dogberry's second speech is even more polite. Negative politeness strategies are employed frequently: expression of deference through *your worship*, which is used four times (+4); the indirect request (*I beseech you*: +2); and a statement of 'self-effacement' (*I humbly*: +1).

Dogberry's second speech contains an offer *if a merry meeting may be wished, God prohibit it*, which is mitigated by negative politeness strategies: it is softened by the conditional force of *if* (+1), the modal *may* hedges the imposition (+1), and there is a passive voice *may be wished*, which adds another point. Negative politeness works by dissociation: in *God prohibit it*, Dogberry dissociates himself and Leonato from a future act that only God can decide (+1). Positive politeness is observed in (*God keep...*, *I wish your worship well*, and *God restore you* (+3). In addition, the offer itself (*if a merry...*) is also a feature of positive politeness, which adds another point. Giving reasons *for the example of others* scores +1.

The second speech thus scores +15 for politeness, as against +5 for the first one. Dogberry is being more polite in his second speech so as to convince Leonato to punish Conrade 'an arrant knave', on whom Dogberry wants to take revenge because when questioned he, first, played the injured, innocent 'toff' and then spoiled everything by calling Dogberry an 'ass' (cf. 4, 2, 60). The massive redress in the second speech corresponds to the extremity of the FTA.

When addressing Margaret in his first speech in (52), Benedick is concerned about being polite because he wants to gain access to Beatrice with Margaret's help: a serious FTA in comparison with the second one. His speech reveals some degree of indirectness, which is expressed by an indirect request softened by *Pray thee*, scoring +1 for deference (negative politeness). Further deference is expressed in the adorned deferential title *sweet Mistress* (+2); in addition, nominalisation occurs (*to the speech of Beatrice*: +1), which gives a total score of +4 just for negative politeness. Benedick's second speech does not display markers of politeness because he is merely giving Margaret a piece of advice as to how to use `the bucklers`: a non-serious FTA. The difference in politeness between the two speeches shows that Benedick surrounds the more serious FTA with supporting means underpinning `rank` as well as increasing its effect.

The third scene in Act I of *Measure for Measure* opens with the first speech in (53), which takes place during a dialogue between Duke Vincentio and Friar Thomas. It can be deduced that Friar Thomas has formed a wrong opinion of the Duke's intention to disguise himself in order to court a lady incognito. The Duke explains that he is not pursuing a lady and that he has a more serious `aim` without revealing what he is really expecting from Friar Thomas, which makes his FTA less risky than the second one. Negative politeness scores +3, +2 for the adorned deferential title *Holy father* and +1 for nominalisation *secret harbor*. As to positive politeness, *more grave and wrinkled* scores +2 for exaggeration, which makes a total score of +5?

In his second speech the Duke's intentions are disclosed. Having decided to disguise himself as a monk and stay in Vienna in order to see what happens after leaving his deputy in charge of affairs, he asks Friar Thomas to `instruct him` how to disguise himself as a true Friar - a serious FTA. Being aware of the extremity of his FTA, the Duke seeks to soften his demand although he is addressing someone with less power. His first speech is characterised by several sub-strategies with components of positive and negative politeness:

Positive politeness strategies include exaggeration (*too dreadful*: +2), showing sympathy (*Twould be my tyranny*: +1), giving reasons (*for we bid them*: +1), using 'in-group identity terms' (*I prithee*: +1) (cf. Brown and Gilman 1989, 184), showing reciprocity (*At our more leisure render you*: +1), and being optimistic (*as twere a brother of your order*: +1). Moreover, the Duke calls upon the 'cooperativeness' of Friar Thomas by including him in the activity, using 'inclusive' forms such as (*we bid, At our more leisure, shall we see, our seemers*: +4). These 'plural forms' seem to suggest a type of 'collaborative' plural rather than a 'regal' one. First, this can be justified by the fact that the Duke does not use the 'collaborative plural' if he wants to attribute negative qualities to his person *twas my fault* and *Twould be my tyranny*. Second, the fact that the Duke makes abundant use of the first person singular (*I do fear, I bid, I will, I may, I read*) seems to support the claim that he uses the plural form only when seeking 'cooperativeness'. Altogether, positive politeness strategies reach a score of +11.

With regard to negative politeness, the Duke starts by expressing deference, which is extended to humbling his capacities (*I do fear, twas my fault, And yet my nature never in the fight to do in slander*), where he admits indirect responsibility for years of lax rule. The Duke also abases himself when he asks the Friar to *instruct* him. Deference through 'self-effacement' gives a score of +4. Further deference occurs in (*my father*: +1). To weaken the impact of his demand, the Duke hedges 'the assumptions and commitments' implicit in his FTA (*Indeed, as it were*: +2), and additional hedges are achieved through the modal verbs (*would, may*: +2). Nominalisation is also at work here, *my fault* acting as a 'formalising device' that removes the Duke from the FTA (+1). Furthermore, the Duke is concerned about minimising his FTA (*Only, this one*: +1). *Lord Angelo is precise* [...] *than stone* is also a feature of negative politeness, where the Duke dissociates himself from the particular imposition in the FTA and softens the offence (+1) (cf. Table 2, strategy 8). Negative politeness strategies thus score +11.

The score for the two strategies combined is +22, which makes this speech one of the politest in *Measure for Measure*. This is successful in that Friar Thomas accedes to the Duke's request. Comparing the unequal extremity in the two speeches, it can be concluded that when the Duke asks Friar Thomas to give him shelter, which is not directly expressed at the beginning of the scene, this is a less extreme threat than when he requires assistance in his disguise as a monk while his people think that he is abroad.

In his first speech in (54), Lucio, trying to convince Isabella to go and 'soften Angelo' for her brother's sake, starts by dissociating himself from the 'intrinsic extremity' of his FTA by implying that he is merely forced to come and impinge on her 'freedom of action' because of the Duke's absence (*The Duke is strangely* [...] *of his authority*: +1) and the cruelty of Angelo (*Governs Lord Angel* [...]. *To make him an example*: +1). Lucio's indirect request (*Unless you have the grace...*) scores +2; the utterance *by your fair prayer*, which also indicates deference by the use of the adjective *fair*, scores +1 for negative politeness, which makes a total score of +5. Having succeeded in minimising his imposition, Lucio, in his second speech, ceases to be polite and addresses Isabella with no courtesy at all. On the contrary, he obliges her to humiliate herself *Kneel down before him*. His 'verbless imperatives' *to him*, used twice, score -2; in addition, he is assuming more power by using the emphatic *I say*. (54) thus consists of two FTAs: the first one is Lucio's polite attempt to convince Isabella. In the second step, which cannot take place unless Isabella has agreed to go to Angelo, Isabella is obeying

Lucio, who now claims the right to impose on her as if he were her social superior. The two FTAs are clearly framed according to the extremity involved.

In (55) Isabella first describes her dilemma, i.e. the conflict between holding her brother's vice in abhorrence and the love she feels for him. The first speech can almost be interpreted as a soliloquy. She appears to be talking to herself, hardly noticing the presence of a hearer. The pronoun `you´ is not used at all, whereas the personal pronoun `I´ shows up five times (*I do abhor*, *I would not*, *I must*, used twice, *I am*). Isabella is not concerned about being polite because the FTA of her speech is intended to arouse Angelo's sympathy. Only when Angelo intervenes *Well, the matter* does she proceed directly to her more serious FTA in the second speech. Her plea is framed by two politeness strategies: first, she claims that she "has compelling reasons for doing the FTA" (*I have a brother is condemned to die*: +1) (Brown and Gilman 1989, 189); second, her indirect request *I do beseech you* adds two points, giving a total score of +3 for negative politeness. The FTA in the second speech is more extreme than the first, and Angelo knows that he is asked to do something so extreme because he is asked too politely.

In (56) Claudio's horror at the thought of death leads him to have no understanding for Isabella's chastity. His plea is mitigated by politeness strategies, aiming at softening the imposition of his FTA, but in vain. *Sweet sister* scores +2 for positive politeness (use in-group identity terms); giving reasons *Nature dispenses with the deed* [...] *a virtue* adds another point for positive politeness. *What sin you do to save a brother's life* minimises the imposition (+1). The total score for his extreme request is (+3). At the rejection of his plea, Claudio, in his state of despair, reacts with a cry. His request to be heard, in his second speech, scores no points for politeness. Clearly enough, the more extreme FTA is the one that is mitigated by politeness strategies.

In (57) the Duke asks the provost to conceal him during the encounter between Claudio and Isabella so that he can overhear them, which is an extreme FTA, though less serious than the FTA in the second speech, in which the Duke, as a Friar, asks the Provost earnestly and politely to delay Claudio's execution. Using politeness strategies, the Duke manages to convince the Provost. He does this by complimenting the Provost with being honest *There is written in your brain, provost, honesty and constancy*, which scores +1 for positive politeness. The compliment is supported by the conditional force of *if* and by the 'adverbial hedge' *truly*, which score +2 for negative politeness. To dissociate himself from the imposition of the FTA, the Duke states his FTA 'as an instance of a general rule' (cf. Table 2, strategy 8) (*Claudio [...] is no greater forfeit to the law than Angelo who hath sentenced him*: +1). Furthermore, the Duke's strategy *but four days' respite* minimises the imposition and adds another point, which makes a total score of +4 for negative politeness. By exaggerating *present and dangerous courtesy*, the Duke's speech adds two points to positive politeness, which gives a total score of +6.

At the start of the Induction to *The Taming of the Shrew* the Lord is, in his first speech (58), concerned about being polite because of the seriousness of his FTA, which involves setting in motion the practical joke of persuading a drunken tinker that he is a nobleman woken up from a fifteen-year sleep. To put his plan into practice, he addresses his servants with the plural deferential title *Sirs*, which scores +1 for negative politeness. His household is also indirectly requested to join him in his trick (*What think you [...] himself?* +1) (negative politeness). Being assured that they are going to join him, the lord, who is unquestionably obeyed by everybody, ceases to be polite and addresses his servants baldly on-record. The command *Take him* scores no points for politeness, and the two 'verbless' imperatives (*to bed with him, each one to his office*: -2) are baldly expressed. The contrast between the two speeches shows that politeness increases with the extremity of the face threat.

Hortensio's first speech in (59) is characterised by its extreme politeness. With respect to negative politeness, his speech scores +3 for giving deference: +1 for the first indirect request *So will I...*, +1 for the second indirect speech *I pray* and +1 for the deferential title *Signor Cremio*. The speech also scores +1 because *but a word* minimises the imposition and +1 for nominalisation *our quarrel*. Furthermore, the two hedges *may* and *happy* add two points; the first one mitigating the imposition implied in the FTA, the second one softening the noun *rivals*, which makes a total score of +7 for negative politeness. As to positive politeness, the items *our quarrel, touched us*, and *our fair mistress* score +3 because by including the hearer in the activity, the speaker "can call upon the cooperative assumptions and thereby redress FTAs" (Brown and Levinson 1987, 127). The total score of the first speech is thus +10. The indirect request with its polite markers is one of the politest speeches in the play. The 'excessive redress' in the first speech suggests that the FTA which Hortensio has in mind is too risky to communicate without polite means.

The conversation continues as follows:

Hortensio   Marry, sir, to get a husband for her sister (1, 1, 117)

The riskier FTA is now disclosed: to find a husband for Katharina because Baptista says no one will marry Bianca until his elder daughter, Katharina, is off his hands.

In his second speech Hortensio is not concerned about being polite because the FTA is not as risky as the first one; Hortensio tries to convince Greme that finding a husband for Katharina is not unrealistic because *there be good fellows* interested in her fortune. The weightiness of the second speech is not as extreme as that of the first one, and this accounts for the higher degree of politeness in the first speech.

In his first speech in (60) Petruchio's motive for his coming to Padua is clear: 'to wive it wealthily'. This justifies his use of politeness when asking Hortensio to find a rich woman for him. Negative politeness can be observed in the deferential title *Signor Hortensio* (+1) and in the indirect request (*if thou know*: +1). As to positive politeness, *such friends* scores +1 for 'in group identity terms' and the inclusive *we* adds another point for a total score of +4 for the first speech. Petruchio's second speech shows that he is only pretending to be dissatisfied with the tailor's work in the presence of Katharina so as to deprive her, during the taming process, of beautiful clothes. Petruchio's behaviour is calculated; this is seen in his aside, where he commands Hortensio to pay the tailor for his work: an FTA that is less risky than the first one. He says *Hortensio* instead of *Signor Hortensio*, and he uses the directive *say* instead of mitigating his FTA with an indirect request, as in the first speech.

It is true that Petruchio is less polite in his second speech; however, the context must be taken into consideration to do him justice. He is in the course of taming Katharina, and he cannot let her notice that she is being cheated. Therefore, the prime reason for his bald on-record usage is to deceive Katharina with 'maximum efficiency'.

Addressing Petruchio this time, Hortensio, in his first speech in (61), wants to disguise himself as a music-teacher, and under the pretence of teaching

Bianca to flirt with her. Petruchio is asked to assist him in his disguise. Being aware of the seriousness of his FTA, Hortensio frames his request with politeness markers. As far as negative politeness is concerned, the speech scores +1 for the indirect request (*Now shall...*), +1 for minimising the imposition *at least*, +1 for the modal *may*, and +2 for its nominalisations *have leave and leisure*, which makes a total score of +5 for negative politeness. Positive politeness scores only +1 for giving reasons *that so I may [...] by herself*, which brings the total politeness score to +6.

In his second speech Hortensio is addressing Petruchio with no courtesy at all because the FTA is not as serious as the first one, i.e. he is only telling Petruchio to admit being defeated when arguing with Tranio. More important, the second speech takes place while the wedding of Katharina and Bianca is celebrated, and such a context allows more familiarity and accounts for the use of the simple imperative *confess*, which is used twice. Clearly enough, the more polite speech is the one containing the more extreme FTA.

In his first speech in (62) Tranio is extravagantly polite owing to the weight of the FTA he has in mind: he is asking the Pedant, an old man brought off the street by Biondello, to play the part of Tranio's/Lucentio's father. As far as negative politeness is concerned, the indirect request (*If this be...*), accessed with the use of the subjunctive *be*, scores +2, and the deferential title *sir*, used twice, adds another two points for deference. Moreover, the speech scores +1 for the passive form *you shall be friendly lodged*, which amounts to a total score of +5 for negative politeness. As to positive politeness, the promise *This favor will I do* scores +1, the offer *And in my house [...] lodged* another +1. In addition, there is a positive politeness hedge *friendly*, which adds another point, which gives a total score of +3 for positive politeness, i.e. +8 altogether. Meanwhile, the Pedant is persuaded to play the role of Vincentio, and Tranio is reassured because his plan seems feasible and the deception perfect, i.e. Tranio no longer needs to be over-polite to the merchant in his second speech. Baldly on-record, he tells the Pedant to keep up his role without panic. Certainly, the ranked extremity of the FTA in the two speeches is quite different, and this accounts for the difference in the degree of politeness invested in the two speeches.

In *Twelfth Night*, in her first speech (63) Viola, shipwrecked and impoverished, decides to disguise herself as a page-boy in order to serve Duke Orsino and improve her situation. To achieve this purpose, she asks Antonio to assist her in her disguise. Viola's FTA is too extreme, but she succeeds in softening its weight. With regard to positive politeness, Viola starts by complimenting Antonio (*There is a fair* [...] *outward character*: +1). In connecting Antonio's nature with his appearance, she states that Antonio's goodly exterior reflects his goodly interior (cf. Donno 1985, 49, n: 48-51). The compliment is hedged by *fair*, used twice (+2), and *beauteous* (+1). Showing reciprocity in her promise *I'll pay thee bounteously* adds another two points. Giving reasons *for such disguise shall become my intent* and *for I can sing* [...] *his service* scores +2, which adds up to a total score of +7 for positive politeness. As to negative politeness, the two indirect requests *I prithee* and *It may be worth thy pains* score +2 for giving deference. The first indirect request is softened by an 'adverbial hedge' (*bounteously*: +1). *Only shape* minimises the imposition (+1), and nominalisations *be my aid* and *thy silence* add another +2, which gives a total score of +6 for negative politeness. Positive politeness and negative politeness together score +13, which makes this speech one of the politest ones in *Twelfth Night*.

Antonio agrees to help Viola, and she soon ceases to be extravagantly polite. Her second speech scores only +1 for positive politeness, expressing gratitude *I thank thee*; otherwise, the command *lead me on* is direct. Furthermore, the FTA in the second speech is not as risky as the first one since Viola merely asks Antonio to go first and show her the way. The two speeches are obviously of unequal extremity.

After dismissing his servants "so that Curio and attendants will not hear his directives to Viola-Cesario" (Donno 1985, 56, n: 11), the Duke begins his first speech in (64) by giving reasons for his FTA: *I have unclasped [...] soul*; this strategy scores +1 for positive politeness. *Good youth* adds two more points: +1 for the positive politeness hedge *good* and another point for *youth*, which, although not an honorific form of address, expresses 'affection' and 'intimacy' (cf. Brown and Gilman 1989, 183-84). More important, *good youth* cannot be an adorned deferential title because Orsino quite often[3] uses the affectionate term of address *boy* when addressing Viola/Cesario. As to negative politeness, the speech scores +2: +1 for nominalisation *thy gait* and +1 for the indirect request *be not denied access*, which Brown and Gilman, following Blake (1983, 98), find that it "is not an action imperative but an agentless passive, which has no presumptions in it" (1989, 160). All these polite markers work together to soften Orsino's FTA that Cesario/Viola should go and carry a love message from him to Olivia. The total politeness score of the first speech is +5. In contrast, Orsino's second speech does not contain markers of politeness, he is simply telling Cesario/Viola which women to choose and pointing to the sensitivity of women.

---

[3] The following are the citations where Cesario/Viola is addressed with the positive politeness term of address 'boy': 2, 4, 13; 2, 4, 23; 2, 4, 30; 2, 4, 115; 5, 1, 118; 5, 1, 66.

In her first speech in (65) Olivia, being suspicious because of Cesario/Viola's use of politeness, tells him/her to reveal what he/she is charged to report: an FTA whose weight is not extreme. Viola's appearance in the guise of Cesario transforms Olivia's personality, and her transition from dominance into ardent passion is reflected in her linguistic behaviour in the second speech. She falls 'headlong' in love with Cesario/Viola and wants him/her never to speak of Orsino any more, which is a serious FTA. In contrast to the first speech, which scores no points for politeness, the second speech contains numerous polite markers. As far as negative politeness is concerned, the first indirect request (*by your leave...*) scores +2; the second indirect request *I pray you*, which stresses the first one, adds another point. By switching from the present into the past *I bade* Olivia distances herself from the 'here and now' and makes her polite FTA seem more remote and thus more polite (cf. Brown and Levinson 1987, 204); this mechanism of negative politeness adds another point. In addition, the use of *would* indicates scepticism (+1), and Olivia's request to switch to another subject matter is softened by the adverbial hedge *rather* (+1), which brings the speech to a total score of +6. The two speeches are scored differently, corresponding to the ranked extremity involved in the two speeches.

In his first speech in (66) Malvolio, imprisoned and left alone as a madman in a 'dark room', is calling Feste, the Clown, baldly on-record. The name *Fool* is not mitigated by any adorned adjectives. On the contrary, to attract Feste's attention Malvolio stresses his FTA by the emphatic *I say*. However, in his second speech he is concerned with being polite because of the seriousness of his FTA: he needs Feste to carry a message to Olivia in order to prove that he is sane. Feste is now addressed with the deferential title *Good Fool*, which scores +1 for negative politeness. By indicating the reciprocal aspect of his FTA *it shall advantage thee more than ever the bearing of letter did*, Malvolio negates 'the debt aspect' of his request (+1), which brings the total politeness score to +2. The second speech, whose FTA is more serious, is framed more politely.

4. 3 Distance

In order to test the effects of the variable distance, "we need two FTAs involving the same two persons with each person staying in speaker or hearer role. Power relations must remain the same; the two FTAs must be matched in extremity, but there must be a clear change in D, which could be a change of affection or interactive closeness or both" (Brown and Gilman 1989, 192).

Play	Congruent with theory[a]	Weakly contradictory to theory[b]	Strongly contradictory to theory[c]	Total
Much Ado about Nothing	0	0	6	6
Measure for Measure	0	0	3	3
Twelfth Night	0	0	3	3
The Taming of the Shrew	0	0	2	2
Total	0	0	14	14

Table 9. Contrasts of distance alone with distance interpreted as 'affect'
  [a] In the case marked by greater positive affect, speech is less polite
  [b] In cases differing in level of politeness positive affect, there is no difference in politeness
  [c] In the case marked by greater positive affect, speech is more polite

As expected, like in the tragedies (cf. Table 5) analysed by Brown and Gilman (1989), the clear instances in the four comedies (cf. Table 9) are all changes of 'affect', i.e. the more two people like one another, the greater their concern with protecting each other's face. Table 9 shows that *Much Ado about Nothing* has exactly twice as many dyads as *Measure for Measure* and *Twelfth Night* (6 versus 3) but three times as many as *The Taming of the Shrew* (6 versus 2). All the 14 contrasts in Table 9 disconfirm Brown and Levinson's framework because in all instances more politeness is used when two individuals like each other, and politeness vanishes when the opposite is the case. Following Slugoski and Turnbull (1988), Brown and Gilman conclude that "[p]oliteness in the plays, in so far as it is governed by D, is governed by feeling; interactive intimacy is of little importance. With the extension of positive feeling (liking or better), the speaker becomes more polite; and if positive feeling is withdrawn (dislike, hostility), the speaker becomes less polite" (1989, 192).

4. 3. 1 Some consequences of the relationship affect variable

In their interaction, participants are expected to conform to Grice's Conversational Maxims and not to threaten one another's face. Accordingly, Slugoski and Turnbull conclude, in agreement with Brown and Levinson (1987), "that the main reason people depart from the CP [Conversational Principle], and hence use indirect constructions for their utterances, is precisely so that they can get their message across while at the same time minimising the potential face-threat of that message" (1988, 103). These two requirements - Gricean Maxims and knowledge of social relationships - are reconciled by Brown and Levinson's formula, repeated here for the sake of clarity:

$$Wx = D(S, H) + P(H, S) + Rx$$

in which they "handle this contingency by relativising the operation of Grice's maxims to specify aspects of the social relationship of the participants" (Slugoski and Turnbull 1988, 103). However, Brown and Levinson's equation does not include an 'affect parameter' because "the formula was, no doubt, written for the kind of familiar case in which acquaintanceship ripens into friendship, interaction grows more intimate and liking increases" (Brown and Gilman 1989, 193). According to Brown and Gilman, it has not yet been shown how such a factor should be integrated into the Brown/Levinson model (ibid., 196).

What Brown and Gilman found in Shakespeare's tragedies is a "change of feeling [...] often extreme and sudden [...]. In these circumstances, the more the speaker likes the hearer, the greater the concern with the hearer's face and so the more polite the speech; the less the liking, the less the concern and also the politeness [...]. Our sources are dramas - Shakespearean tragedies - and the changes of feeling enacted in them are sudden and dramatic" (ibid., 193-5). In the comedies the same change of feelings is observed; it is also extreme and sudden. Therefore, politeness in the comedies also depends on affection, i.e. politeness vanishes when affection is withdrawn, and it returns with the return of affection. However, many speeches defy pairing because the character may be in a state of rage. Two passages involving states of furious speech have already been discussed, one from *Hamlet* and the other from *Measure for Measure* (cf. 2. 2. 2). States of rage occur, however, quite often in the comedies in question; that is why it is very important to quote two other pairs. For instance, it is not possible to make a pair of Katharina (*The Taming of the Shrew*) saying:

> KATHARINA (politely begging Petruchio's servant for some food)
>   I like it well: good Grumio, fetch it me.
>   (4, 3, 21)
> KATHARINA (furiously scolding Grumio for depriving her of food)
>   Go, get thee gone, thou false deluding slave,
>   [Beats him]
>   That feed'st me with the very name [only the name] of meat:
>   Sorrow on thee and all the pack of you,
>   That triumph thus upon my misery!
>   Go, get thee gone, I say.
>   (4, 3, 31-35)
>   [Enter PETRUCHIO and HORTENSIO with meat]

Nor is it possible to pair the two speeches from *Twelfth Night*:

> OLIVIA   (affectionately wondering at Sir Toby's deplorable state)
>   Cousin, cousin, how have you come so early by this lethargy?
>   (1, 5, 102)
> OLIVIA   (furiously blaming Sir Toby for harming
>   Cesario, whom she loves)

> Will it be ever thus? Ungracious wretch,
> Fit for the mountains and the barbarous caves,
> Where manners ne'er were preached! out of my sight!
> Be not offended, dear Cesario.
> Rudesby, be gone!
> [Exeunt SIR TOBY BELCH, SIR ANDREW, and FABIAN]
> I prithee, gentle friend,
> Let thy fair wisdom, not thy passion, sway
> In this uncivil and thou unjust extent
> Against thy peace. Go with me to my house,
> And hear thou there how many fruitless pranks
> This ruffian hath botch'd up, that thou thereby
> Mayst smile at this: thou shalt not choose but go:
> Do not deny. Beshrew his soul for me,
> He started one poor heart of mine in thee.
> (4, 1, 40-54)

4. 3. 2 Contrasts of distance as affect

The first speech in (67) was already discussed with respect to the variable rank (R); it is now reconsidered in terms of `affect´. The speech scores +5: +3 for positive politeness and +2 for negative politeness, cf. the second speech in dyad (48). The interesting aspect is its positive politeness, which is observed in particular in *my dear son*. *My son* scores +1 for "positive politeness (4): Use in-group identity terms" (Brown and Gilman 1989, 184), and the positive politeness hedge *dear* adds another point for a total score of +2. The politeness of the speech reflects Leonato's positive feelings towards Claudio. Meanwhile, Claudio is misled into believing that Hero is disloyal and accuses her of unfaithfulness; she faints, and the wedding is interrupted. Leonato, Hero's father, is heartbroken and becomes hostile to Claudio. This change of attitude accounts for the withdrawal of positive feeling in his second speech, where "Leonato uses the familiar and (in this situation) contemptuous second person singular to address Claudio, and maintains this until his exit" (Mares 1988, 127, n: 53). Moreover, the `isolated thou of contempt´ in *thou dissembler, thou* scores another -1. The elimination of politeness and the withdrawal of positive feelings in the second speech go hand in hand.

(68) shows a similar contrast. The first speech results from Margaret's successive disagreements with Hero about what Hero should wear during the wedding. She has a negative evaluation of Hero's positive face since she thinks that her choice is wrong and unreasonable, and such wrongness is associated with disapproval. Margaret's FTA leads Hero to have no concern for Margaret's face. She cries *Fie upon thee! art not ashamed?*, i.e. Margaret ought to be ashamed of herself. However, Hero's second speech, where Margaret is not the only person addressed, scores +2 for positive politeness as far as Margaret is concerned: +1 for the hedge *good* and another point for the diminutive *Meg*. Brown and Levinson identify diminutivised terms of address and endearment as 'in-group identity' markers through which the speaker can implicitly claim 'in-group' solidarity with the addressee (1987, 107-8). Therefore, the second speech shows that the return of good feelings and affection leads Hero to resume politeness.

A few points are still worthy of remark with regard to Hero's language. In the four plays in question, the politeness which is observed in the use of the diminutives *coz* for cousin, *Meg* for Margaret, and *Ursley* for Ursula (cf. 3, 1, 4) is not found in a male speech. It is true that Gremio uses the diminutive *youngling* in *The Taming of the Shrew* (cf. 2, 1, 326), but it is meant to belittle his competitor, Tranio/Lucentio, so as to win Bianca's love, cf. dyad (77). As far as the suffix -*ling* is concerned, "[w]here the referent is human, the formation is somewhat contemptuous" (Quirk et al. 1985, 1549). Hence, the double function of diminutives, i.e. to communicate either affection and tenderness or criticism. It could be argued that women's talk seems to be more affective than that of men and that women are thus more likely to employ positive politeness strategies than men. If this is true, then a gender variable should be taken into consideration when dealing with politeness: a point not discussed by Brown and Gilman, who blindly follow Brown and Levinson's model in this respect.

In his first speech in (69) Claudio believes that Hero is unfaithful. He has no concern for her face and even threatens to make a 'public exposure' of the accusations brought against her (cf. Mares 1988, 112, n: 50). In sum, Claudio's dislike of Hero is responsible for the elimination of the 'apparatus of politeness'. However, when he discovers that Hero is falsely accused, Claudio changes his mind and speaks softly, saying *Sweet Hero*. The selection of the positive politeness hedge *sweet* (+1) supports the assumption that politeness is associated with positive feelings towards the addressee.

Obeying Beatrice's instructions, Benedick, in his first speech in (70), accuses Claudio of having caused Hero's death *you have killed a sweet lady* and challenges him to a duel *I will make it good how you dare [...] or I will protest your cowardice*. Like Edgar, who challenges his brother, Edmund, to a duel as well (cf. *King Lear*, 5, 3, 127), Benedick is intense but not furious, and his dislike for Claudio accounts for his impoliteness. As soon as Borachio is arrested and confesses, Benedick no longer dislikes Claudio, as the return of affection in the second speech clearly shows. The speech reveals a striking preference for positive politeness, which, first, occurs in the repeated use of the directives (*come, come*: +1) which have a positive connotation. Second, the inclusion of the hearer in the activity (*we*, used three times, *our*, used twice, and *let's*) adds another +6; third, the speech scores +1 for using the 'in-group identity' term *friends*. Fourth, giving reasons *that we may lighten our own hearts, and our wives' heels* increases the total score to +9 for positive politeness. Negative politeness, on the other hand, scores only +1 for the modal hedge *may*, which brings the speech to a total score of +10. Clearly enough, the two matched speeches show that the advent of good feelings is accompanied with increased politeness.

Being treated as a villain and challenged to a duel by Leonato (cf. 5, 1, 58-71), Claudio's regard for Leonato's face vanishes and with it affection and politeness as well. In (71), Claudio's speech scores -1 for the 'verbless imperative' *away*. However, the events move to reconciliation, for Dogberry, the chief constable, manages to reveal the truth by leading Conrade to confess that Don John, Don Pedro's bastard brother, is responsible for Hero's disgrace and the breaking-off of her engagement to Claudio. As a result, the coming of positive feelings calls for greater politeness 'investment'. Positive politeness scores +2: +1 for the interjection *O* and another point for the compliment *your overkindness*. As to negative politeness, the speech scores +4: +2 for the deferential title *noble sir* and +2 for 'self-effacement' *wring tears from me* and *poor Claudio*, where Claudio humbles himself. Altogether, positive politeness and negative politeness reach a score of +6 in Claudio's second speech, in which politeness and affection go hand in hand.

The first speech in (72) was already discussed when the variable power (P) was dealt with. It scores +2 for positive politeness; negative politeness, on the other hand, is not present, cf. the second speech in dyad (1). This means that 'familiarity' and 'solidarity' serve to deepen the good relationship still existing between Don Pedro and Leonato. Such a relationship of shared positive feelings is clearly observed when Don Pedro suggests that they go hand in hand *give me your hand*. To be more precise, the politeness level is very high, and this implies a high level of affection, i.e. positive feelings. When Don Pedro is duped into believing that he sees Hero affectionately receiving Borachio in her chamber (in fact it is not Hero but Margaret), he charges her with unfaithfulness, thinking that there is 'very good proof' of the accusation against her. The incident thus changes the relationship between Don Pedro and Leonato, Hero's father. The withdrawal of positive feelings is the prime reason for Don Pedro's impoliteness in his second speech, where he addresses Leonato contemptuously with *old man*, showing no concern for his face. In addition, Don Pedro's disagreement *you are not right* proves that he now has a negative evaluation of Leonato's face. Clearly enough, politeness vanishes with the withdrawal of positive feelings.

In his first speech in (73) the Duke is polite to Angelo as the 'extension of affection' predicts. Among the items which depict the politeness of the speech compliments occur four times: the Duke compliments Angelo's personality *a kind of character* (+1), his achievements *Thy history* (+1), and his qualities *belongings* (+1). The strategy of making compliments reaches its heights in (*But I do bend my speech to one that can my part in him advertise*: +1) where the Duke says that he does not need to address "one who knows more about governing in my place than I can tell him" (Gibbons 1991, 81, n: 40-1). Moreover, the fact that the Duke chooses Angelo as a deputy (*In our remove be thou at full ourself*: +1) is an act of promotion, which indicates the Duke's approval of Angelo. The total score for positive politeness is thus +5. Besides, the Duke does not only make use of the 'royal plural' *Heaven doth with us as we, As if we had, In our remove be at ourself* but also of the 'ordinary' first person singular *But I do bend*, thus lessening the asymmetry power relation.

The Duke, while pretending to leave the city, in fact remains there in disguise and discovers how cruelly Angelo rules the country. When he throws off his disguise, he unmasks Angelo in the trial scene, in which the Duke is no longer concerned with being polite to him since his plan is to destroy Angelo through Isabella's denunciation. The second speech testifies the Duke's negative feelings towards Angelo, i.e. he has no concern for his face. As Reploge argues "[a] loss of position [...] was followed by a diminution of honour [...]. It is to be expected, then, that plays which deal with the fall of men from positions of power will reflect this in changes in names and titles" (1973, 178). Angelo's downfall and 'diminution of honor' are therefore reflected in the Duke's second speech: (*whose salt imagination yet hath wronged, Angelo thy fault's thus manifested; which, though thou wouldst deny denies thee vantage)*; in addition, there is a 'verbless imperative' *Away with him* (-1). In contrast to the first speech, where both the 'royal plural' and the first person singular are used, the second speech displays only the 'royal plural' *We do condemn thee*, thus assuming more power. Clearly enough, the withdrawal of positive feelings is accompanied by the elimination of politeness.

In her first encounter with Angelo (cf. Act 2, Scene 2) Isabella confronts him with successive speeches aimed at convincing him to temper justice with mercy. When she is assured that he will change his mind because he tells her to come again the next day *well; come to me tomorrow* (cf. 2, 2, 160), she is relieved and led to hope that he will spare her brother's life. Her hopes are also raised by Lucio encouraging her to be optimistic *Go to. 'Tis well. Away* (cf. 2, 2, 161). Isabella's optimism leads to positive feelings towards Angelo, which are expressed in her first speech in (74). It scores +1 for positive politeness because she asks God's favour for Angelo *Heaven keep your honour safe* and +1 for the deferential title *your honour* (negative politeness). Isabella is soon disappointed when Angelo rejects her plea: he agrees to save her brother's life only if she sleeps with him (cf. 2, 4, 160-68). Shocked by Angelo, who neither takes into account her feelings about virginity nor her vocation as a nun, she reacts with a speech in which she threatens to denounce him. Isabella becomes intense and ardent, and her negative feelings account for her impoliteness, i.e. *Ha! little honour*, as against *your honour* in the first speech, *Seeming, seeming*, the use of the name *Angelo* with no adorned adjective, and the commands *Look for't* and *sign me*. The two speeches demonstrate that Isabella becomes impolite because positive feelings have been eliminated.

Lucio's speech in (75) takes place while he is slandering the Duke to 'Friar Lodowick', not realising that they are one and the same person. When 'Friar Lodowick' contradicts Lucio's slanders against the Duke *Tis not possible* (cf. 3, 2, 109), Lucio rejects the contradiction, telling the 'Friar' that he is *deceived*. Nevertheless, he remains polite. His speech scores +1 for the interjection *Oh* (positive politeness) and +1 for the deferential title *sir* (negative politeness); in addition, there is a passive form *you are deceived*, which adds another point to negative politeness, producing a total score of +3. However, when the 'Friar' threatens to reveal everything, Lucio turns on him in consequence of his change of feelings. His dislike for the 'Friar' is reflected in his second speech, in which he accuses him of slandering the Duke. Negative feelings towards the 'Friar' can further be observed in the 'isolated' *thou* (-1) and in the insult *damnable fellow*. Lucio is not furious but intense because the period of time between the threat (cf. 3, 2, 139) and his second speech is long enough to calm him down. Thus, his transition from politeness to impoliteness can be blamed on the 'affect' factor.

In his first speech in (76) Lucentio's servant, pretending to be Lucentio, politely claims the right to court Baptista's daughter, Bianca. The indirect request *I pray* scores +1 for deference, and the deferential title *sir* adds another point, producing a total score of +2 for negative politeness. So far, politeness, which expresses concern for the hearer, is still at play. However, the dispute that results from Baptista's decision to 'sell' his daughter to the highest bidder changes Tranio/Lucentio's feelings towards Gremio, a 'pantalon'. In fact, they become competitors for Bianca's love, and this accounts for his dislike of Gremio, expressed in *Graybeard*, which expresses no regard for Gremio's old age. Moreover, Gremio's love is described as being too cold *thy love doth freeze*, suggesting that he is impotent. In sum, the impoliteness of the second speech is to be attributed to the withdrawal of positive feelings.

(77), which also involves Gremio and Tranio/Lucentio, shows a similar contrast, but the two characters change roles. Trying to outbid Tranio in an auction for Bianca's love and losing (cf. 2, 1, 370-2), Gremio breaks in with *Sirrah*: a contemptuous form of address, scoring -1 for politeness. His dislike of Tranio also shows in *young gamester* and *toy*, in the ironic use of the 'in-group identity terms' *my boy*, and in his telling Tranio to live on his charity *set foot under thy table*. Moreover, he abuses Tranio/Lucentio's father (*your father were a fool...*). Gremio's negative feelings towards Tranio/Lucentio thus feed his use of impoliteness.

In his second speech, strangely enough, Gremio's hostility is not revealed. On the contrary, he describes Petruchio's behaviour before the priest as if he and Tranio/Lucentio were real friends, even employing the deferential title *Sir* (+1) (negative politeness). Positive politeness, on the other hand, is observed when Gremio quotes the priest's 'strong' interjection (*Ay, by gogs-wounds*: +1). The politeness of the second speech is to be attributed to the return of positive feelings towards the addressee.

The first speech in (78) shows that the 'book' of the Duke's 'secret soul' is really unclasped to Cesario/Viola. It also reflects Orsino's political immaturity since a duke is not expected to be so emotional to a page-boy as to elevate him above his appropriate status. However, the speech is very significant with regard to the factor 'affect' because of its display of positive feelings, which are accompanied by the use of politeness. More important, only positive politeness is present, i.e. the tendency towards 'solidarity' and 'common ground'. First, the interjection *O* scores +1; second, *fellow* adds another point for the use of an 'in-group identity' term. Third, the inclusive *we* (+1) brings the speech to a total score of +3. However, when Orsino is told that Cesario/Viola is Olivia's husband, he feels deceived, thinking that Cesario/Viola has courted Olivia for him/herself. This accounts for his use of the contemptuous male form of address *sirrah* (-1), as against the positive politeness term of address *boy* (cf. n: 3), which Orsino frequently uses when addressing Cesario/Viola. The withdrawal of positive feelings thus governs the impoliteness of the second speech.

In (79) Orsino, tired of sending unsuccessful love messages to Olivia, decides to settle the matter himself instead. Upon meeting her, he addresses her politely with the deferential title *Gracious Olivia*, which scores +1 for negative politeness. However, when she openly refuses to accept his suit and hurts his pride, by saying *still so constant* (cf. 5, 1, 100), he becomes hostile but not furious. The withdrawal of positive feelings thus leads to the elimination of the 'apparatus' of politeness; Olivia is no longer addressed with the courtesy corresponding to her social status. Orsino's incivility is clearly apparent in his impolite act to Olivia *you uncivil lady*, as against *Gracious Olivia*, when she was treated with deference. In the second speech Orsino shows that he has no concern for her positive face. The two matched speeches clearly show that politeness is associated with positive feelings and its elimination with negative ones.

In his first speech in (80) Malvolio's rebuke of the Clown (*Such a barren rascal, I saw him* [...] *with another fool*, and *out of his guard*) dismisses positive feelings. He is jealous of Olivia's approval of the Clown, and this accounts for his impoliteness. However, Malvolio's attitude towards Feste changes as a result of his downfall: in the 'letter-intrigue' Malvolio is tricked into believing that Olivia is in love with him and encouraged to appear before her in 'yellow stockings'. Olivia reacts indignantly and has him arrested as a madman. Malvolio's fall brings about his change of attitude towards Feste. Being imprisoned, he is forced to beg even Feste, despised in the first speech, to pity him. The withdrawal of negative feelings thus calls for the use of polite strategies in the second speech. First, *good fool* scores +2: +1 for the positive politeness hedge *good* and another point for showing familiarity *fool*. Second, giving reasons *I am as well [...] in Illyria* adds another point, producing a total of +3 for positive politeness.

The examples treated under 4.3.2 have shown that a change in attitude changes the degree of politeness: negative feelings reduce the use of politeness; with the advent of positive feelings, the speaker resumes politeness, which is expressed in particular through positive politeness. Here, the emphasis is on the 'common grounds' between the characters; this is why it is important to distinguish between negative and positive politeness strategies. Table 10 reports the number of positive and negative politeness strategies used in the polite speech, distance being interpreted as 'affect'. It shows that the speaker tends to prefer positive politeness strategies to negative ones (33 versus

Contrasts of distance as `affect´	Positive Politeness	Negative politeness
67	3	2
68	1	0
69	2	0
70	9	1
71	2	4
72	2	0
73	5	0
74	1	1
75	1	2
76	0	2
77	1	1
78	3	0
79	0	1
80	3	0
Total	33	14

Table 10. Positive and negative politeness strategies used in the polite speech in the contrasts of distance as `affect´

14). In fact, the speaker is not concerned with expressing deference (negative politeness) when trying to establish a framework of familiarity and solidarity. On the contrary, there is emphasis on positive feelings towards the addressee, i.e. the speaker likes the hearer. Here politeness is not primarily a matter of deference, but rather of the extension of affection, which can best be expressed through positive politeness.

5 Conclusion

This study has investigated the way in which Brown and Levinson's politeness theory as modified by Brown and Gilman can be employed in the analysis of dramatic texts. The focus was on the politeness strategies used in Shakespeare's four comedies *Much Ado about Nothing*, *Measure for Measure*, *The Taming of the Shrew*, and *Twelfth Night*. The way the three variables function is very similar to what Brown and Gilman found in the tragedies.

With regard to the variable power (P), the number of contrasts in the four tragedies (cf. Table 3) is considerably higher than in the four comedies (57 versus 46: cf. Table 6). A large difference is detected in contrasts confirming the theory: 50 in the four tragedies as against 37 in the four comedies. Weakly contradictory contrasts both show a total score of three, while strongly contradictory ones score slightly higher in the four tragedies (6 versus 4).

As to the variable rank (R), the four comedies (cf. Table 8) score slightly higher than the four tragedies (20 versus 19: cf. Table 4). All 20 contrasts in the four comedies are congruent with the theory; while one contrast out of 19 in the four tragedies is weakly contradictory.

Affection, which is thought of as the distance (D) of politeness, provides 14 contrasts in the four comedies (cf. Table 9) as against only nine in the four tragedies (cf. Table 5). Only strongly contradictory contrasts were found, which replicates Brown and Gilman's results for the tragedies.

In sum, the outcomes of the variables power (P) and rank (R) function as Brown and Levinson's theory predicts, but the variable distance does not. Instead, a reformulation of Brown and Levinson's politeness theory is called for. Introducing the variable 'affect' is required in the comedies as well.

With regard to the total number of contrasts, the tragedies provide some 6% more contrasts than the comedies (85 versus 80), the variable power (P) being most strongly responsible for such a difference (57 versus 46). However, the number of the power (P) `outcomes´ in the comedies could be less than (46) if *Measure for Measure*, which alone provides (18) instances, were not included. This indicates that *Measure for Measure* does not quite fit into the group of comedies, as the introduction to this study anticipates. As a `problem play´, *Measure for Measure* contains `tragi-comedy´ elements, which makes it difficult to give the play its proper mode, but in terms of the power (P) `outcomes´ the play is closer to the tragedies than to the comedies. One of the touching tragic elements in *Measure for Measure* seems to be Angelo's downfall. When he discovers that all his transgressions are witnessed by the `Duke-in-disguise´, he begs for `immediate sentence´ and `sequent death´ (cf. 5, 1, 366). That he is denied this and is instead forced to marry his cast-off fiancée, Mariana, his possessions being confiscated, is tragedy, not comedy.

To go on arguing about the genre classification of *Measure for Measure* would transcend the scope of this book, but it suffices to say that the application of politeness theory to literary dialogue can contribute to solving literary questions.

When dealing with the variable power, it was demonstrated that the speech from the lower person reveals a striking preference for negative politeness so that a distance relationship, based on deference, remains established, whereas the higher person tends to prefer positive politeness because the risk of `face loss´ to a subordinate is relatively low (cf. Table 7). However, the results of the variable `affect´, which seems to take the place of social distance, show that there is a great tendency towards positive politeness, which expresses 'friendliness' as against the deferential aspect of negative politeness (cf. Table 10). The scoring system advanced by Brown and Gilman proved to be applicable although sometimes it did not resist criticism because, for instance, the apparent politeness may well be irony, cf. dyads (15) and (40). Gender is ignored by Brown and Gilman, i.e. they do not distinguish between men and women when analysing the character's verbal behaviour. In the comedies women are more inclined to use diminutives (positive politeness) than men unless the use of a diminutive is meant to criticise the addressee. Hence, the variable gender (G) is also relevant to politeness theory and should be given a place in the model.

The application of Brown and Levinson's theory, as a discourse model, to dramatic texts has shown that literary dialogue offers a wide social scope, transmitting the colloquial spoken language of the period. Moreover, dramatic dialogue gives the analyst access to unspoken thoughts by providing the text with soliloquies, which reveal the character's true feelings and intentions when an FTA is too risky to be expressed at all (super-strategy 4). This covers the psychological aspect of politeness theory.

Finally, "studying a dramatic text with politeness in mind has much in common with studying protocols of spontaneous child speech with a grammar and a theory of acquisition in mind" (Brown and Gilman 1989, 208).

6. References

Barnet, S., ed. 1963. *Macbeth* (Signet Classic Shakespeare). New York: New American Library.

Brown, R. & A. Gilman. 1960. "The pronouns of power and solidarity". In T.A. Seboek, ed. *Style in Language*. Cambridge, Mass: MIT Press, 253-76.

_____. 1989. "Politeness theory and Shakespeare's tragedies". In *Language and Society* 18: 159-212

Brown, P. & S. Levinson. 1978. *Universals in Language Usage: Politeness Phenomena*. In E. N. Goody, ed. *Questions and Politeness: strategies in social interaction.* Cambridge: Cambridge University Press.

_____. 1987. *Politeness: Some Universals in Language Usage*. Cambridge: Cambridge University Press.

Clark, H. H. & D.H. Schunk. 1980. "Polite response to polite requests". *Cognition* 8: 111-43.

Donno, E. S., ed. 1985. *Twelfth Night* (The New Cambridge Shakespeare) Cambridge: Cambridge University Press.

Fox, L., ed. 1988. *The Shakespearean Handbook*: (*The Essential Companion to Shakespeare's Works, Life and Time*). London: Bodley Head.

Fraser, R., ed. 1963. *King Lear* (Signet Classic Shakespeare). New York: New American Library.

Gibbons, B., ed. 1991. *Measure for Measure* (The New Cambridge Shakespeare). Cambridge: Cambridge University Press

Goffman, E. 1967. *Interaction Ritual: Essays on Face to Face Behaviour.* Garden City: New York.

Grice, H.P. 1975. "Logic and Conversation". In Cole, P & J. L Morgan, eds. *Syntax and Semantics, III: Speech Acts*. New York: Academic, 41-58.

Huber, E., ed. 1963. *Hamlet* (Signet Classic Shakespeare). New York: New American Library.

Kendall, M. B. 1981. "Toward a semantic approach to terms of address: a critique of
    deterministic models in socioliguistics". *Language and Communication* 1: 237-54.

Kernan, A., ed. 1963. *Othello* (Signet Classic Shakespeare). New York: New American Library.

Lakoff, R. T. 1973. "The logic of politeness; or minding your p's and q's". In *Papers*
    from the ninth regional meeting of the Chicago Linguistic Society, 292-305.

Leech, G. N. 1983. *Principles of Pragmatics*. Longman: London.

Mares, F. H., ed. 1988. *Much Ado about Nothing* (The New Cambridge Shakespeare). Cambridge: Cambridge University Press.

Prouty, C. T. 1950. *The Sources of `Much Ado about Nothing'*. Yale: Yale University Press

Quirk, R., G. Greenbaum & J. Svartvik. 1985. *A Comprehensive Grammar of Contemporary English Language*. London: Longman.

Reploge, C. 1973. "Shakespeare's salutations: a study in stylistic etiquette". *Studies in Philology* 70: 172-86. (Reprinted in Salmon, V & E. Burness, eds. 1987. *A reader in the language of Shakesperian drama*. Amsterdam and Philadelphia: John Benjamins, 101-15)

Scollon, R. & B.K. Scollon. 1983. "Face in interethnic communication". In Jack C. Richards & Richards W. Schmidt, ed. *Language and Communication.* London: Longman, 156-188.

Short, M. (1989). "Discourse Analysis and the Analysis of Drama". In Roland Carter & Paul Simpson , eds. *Language Discourse and Literature*: *An Introductory Reader in Discourse Stylistics*. London: UNWIN HYMAN, 139-70

Slugoski, B. & W. Turnball. 1988. "Cruel to be kind and kind to be cruel: sarcasm, banter and social relations". *Journal of Language and social Phsychology* 7: 101-21.

Thompson, A., ed. 1984. *The Taming of the Shrew* (The New Cambridge Shakespeare). Cambridge: Cambridge University Press.

Turner, R. K.1975. "The text of *Twelfth Night*". *Shakespeare Quarterly* 26: 128-38

7 Appendix

The edition quoted from is The New Cambridge Shakespeare: *Much Ado about Nothing* (Mares 1988), *Measure for Measure* (Gibbons 1991), *The Taming of the Shrew* (Thompson 1984), and *Twelfth Night* (Donno 1985).

Contrasts of power (*P*) alone

Much Ado about Nothing

(1) LEONATO (inviting Don Pedro to lead the way)
    Please it your grace lead on?
    (1, 1, 117)
  DON PEDRO (offering his hand modestly)
    Your hand, Leonato; we will go together.
    (1, 1, 118)

(2) DON PEDRO (inquiring firmly for the reasons why Benedick and Claudio did not join the others at Leonato's)
    What secret hath held you here, that you followed not to Leonato's?
    (1, 1, 151-52)
  BENEDICK (begging Don Pedro to spare him an answer)
    I would your grace would constrain me to tell.
    (1, 1, 153)

(3) DON JOHN (expressing his wrath and jealousy of Claudio, his yearning for revenge, and making sure that he can rely on Conrade and Borachio's assistance)
    Come, come, let us thither: this may prove food to my displeasure. That young start-up [upstart] hath all the glory of my overthrow: if I can cross him any way, I bless myself every way. You are both sure [trusty], and will assist me?
    (1, 3, 47-50)
  CONRADE (expressing his total commitment to his master)
    To the death, my lord.
    (1, 3, 51)

(4) DON PEDRO (asking Beatrice in jest whether she would accept him as husband)
    Will you have me, lady?
    (2, 1, 248)
  BEATRICE (humbly replying that her social status is lower than his)
    No, my lord, unless I might have another for working-days: your grace is too costly to wear every day. But, I beseech your grace, pardon me: I was born to speak all mirth and no matter [jokingly and never seriously.
    (2, 1, 248-251)

(5) BENEDICK (commanding his servant to bring him a book)
                 In my chamber window lies a book, bring it hither to me in the orchard.
                 (2, 3, 3-4)
     Boy   (responding obediently)
                 I am here already, sir.
                 (2, 3, 5)

(6) HERO   (preparing to trick Beatrice by letting her overhear how much Benedick loves her)
                 Good Margaret, run thee to the parlor;
                 There shalt thou find my cousin Beatrice
                 Proposing [conversing] with the prince and Claudio:
                 Whisper her ear and tell her, I and Ursley [the familiar pronunciation of Ursula]
                 Walk in the orchard and our whole discourse
                 Is all of her; say that thou overheard'st us;
                 And bid her steal into the pleached bower,
                 Where honeysuckles, ripen'd by the sun,
                 Forbid the sun to enter, like favourites,
                 Made proud by princes, that advance their pride
                 Against that power that bred it: there will she hide her,
                 To listen our purpose. This is thy office;
                 Bear thee well in it and leave us alone.
                 (3, 1, 1-13)
    MARGARET   (expressing her compliance to carry out Hero's order)
                 I'll make her come, I warrant you, presently.
                 (3, 1, 14)

(7) DON PEDRO (announcing his intention to stay only until the wedding ceremony is complete))
                 I do but stay till your marriage be consummate, and
                 then go I toward Arragon.
                 (3, 2, 1-2)
    CLAUDIO   (offering to accompany Don Pedro till Arragon)
                 I'll bring [escort] you thither, my lord, if you'll vouchsafe me.
                 (3, 2, 3)

(8) DON JOHN (requesting permission to talk to his brother, Don Pedro)
                 If your leisure served, I would speak with you.
                 (3, 2, 63-64)
    DON PEDRO (abruptly asking whether he has something personal to talk about before dismissing Claudio)
                 In private?
                 (3, 2, 65)

(9) HERO   (sending Ursula to wake up her cousin, Beatrice, and tell her to come)
                 Good Ursula, wake my cousin Beatrice, and desire her to rise.
                 (3, 4, 1)
    URSULA   (obediently going to perform Hero's order)

          I will, lady.
          (3, 4, 2)

(10) DOGBERRY (asking Leonato to have the arrested persons judged
          before him)
          One word, sir: our watch, sir, have indeed
          comprehended [apprehended] two aspicious [suspicious] persons, and we would have them this morning examined before your worship.
          (3, 5, 35-7)
     LEONATO (granting Dogberry permission to examine the arrested
          persons himself for lack of time)
          Take their examination yourself and bring it me: I
          am now in great haste, as it may appear unto you.
          (3, 5, 37-40)

Measure for Measure

(11) DUKE VINCENTIO (calling for Escalus)
          Escalus.
          (1, 1, 1)
     ESCALUS (obediently responding to the call)
          My lord.
          (1, 1, 2)

(12) ANGELO (attempting to resist his appointment as a deputy)
          Now, good my lord,
          Let there be some more test made of my metal [natural vigour],
          Before so noble and so great a figure
          Be stamp'd upon it.
          (1,1, 47-50)
     DUKE VINCENTIO (rejecting Angelo's proposal for a test by not
          allowing any questioning of his decision)
          No more evasion:
          We have with a leavened [matured] and prepared choice
          Proceeded to you; therefore take your honours.
          Our haste from hence is of so quick condition [urgent nature]
          That it prefers [gives priority] itself and leaves unquestioned
          Matters of needful value [important enough to require attention].
          We shall write to you, As time and our concernings [affairs] shall
          importune How it goes with us, and do look to know
          What doth befall you here. So, fare you well;
          To the hopeful [promting good hopes] execution do I leave you
          Of your commissions.
          (1, 1, 47-60)

(13) ANGELO (explaining to Escalus how the law should be enforced and
          refusing to grant him permission to meddle in his affairs)
          'Tis one thing to be tempted, Escalus,
          Another thing to fall. I not deny,
          The jury, passing [passing judgement] on the prisoner's life,

>   May in the sworn twelve have a thief or two
>   Guiltier than him they try. What's open made to justice,
>   That justice seizes: what know the laws
>   That thieves do pass on thieves? 'Tis very pregnant [evident],
>   The jewel that we find, we stoop and take't
>   Because we see it; but what we do not see
>   We tread upon, and never think of it.
>   You may not so extenuate his offence
>   For I have had such faults; but rather tell me,
>   When I, that censure him, do so offend,
>   Let mine own judgment [sentence on Claudio] pattern out my
>   death,
>   And nothing come in partial. Sir, he must die.
>   (2, 1, 17-31)
> ESCALUS (obediently responding to Angelo's command)
>   Be it as your wisdom will.
>   (2, 1, 32)

(14) ANGELO (asking for the reasons of Elbow's coming with two arrested persons)
> How now, sir! What's your name? and what's the matter?
> (2, 1, 44)

ELBOW (identifying himself before announcing his arrest of
 Pompey and Froth)
> If it please your honour, I am the poor duke's
> constable, and my name is Elbow: I do lean upon [depend on]
> justice, sir, and do bring in here before your good
> honour two notorious benefactors.
> (2, 1, 45-47)

(15) ESCALUS (ironically thanking Pompey before warning him that he will be severely punished if he turns up before him again)
> Thank you, good Pompey; and, in requital of your
> prophecy, hark you: I advise you, let me not find
> you before me again upon any complaint whatsoever;
> no, not for dwelling where you do: if I do, Pompey,
> I shall beat you to your tent, and prove a shrewd [severe]
> Caesar to you; in plain dealing, Pompey, I shall
> have you whipt: so, for this time, Pompey, fare you well.
> (2, 1, 210-215)

POMPEY (ironically expressing his thanks)
> I thank your worship for your good counsel:
> [Aside]
> But I shall follow it as the flesh and fortune shall
> better determine.
> Whip me? No, no; let carman [carter] whip his jade:
> The valiant heart is not whipt out of his trade.
> (2,1, 216-20)
> [Exit]

(16) ANGELO (warning to dismiss the Provost from his office if he does not mind

	his own business)
	Go to; let that be mine [enough: that is for me to decide]:
	Do you your office, or give up your place,
	And you shall well be spared.
	(2,2, 12-14)
Provost	(begging forgiveness and asking what is going to be done with the pregnant Juliet)
	I crave your honour's pardon.
	What shall be done, sir, with the groaning [in labour] Juliet?
	She's very near her hour [of giving birth].
	(2, 2, 15-17)

(17) ISABELLA (humbly requesting permission to be heard)
        I am a woeful suitor to your honour,
        Please but your honour hear me.
        (2, 2, 28-29)

    ANGELO (granting her permission to speak)
        Well; what's your suit?
        (2, 2, 30)

(18) POMPEY (miserably appealing to Lucio for bail)
        I hope, sir, your good worship will be my bail.
        (3, 2, 64)

    LUCIO (carelessly refusing to help Pompey by mocking him)
        No, indeed, will I not, Pompey; it is not the wear.
        I will pray, Pompey, to increase your bondage: If
        you take it not patiently, why, your mettle is the
        more. Adieu, trusty Pompey. 'Bless you, friar.
        (3, 2, 65-68)

(19) ABHORSON (contemptuously agreeing to have Pompey as a deputy
        Come on, bawd; I will instruct thee in my trade; follow.
        (4, 2, 43)

    POMPEY (expressing his interest in his new post and his readiness to do something in return)
        I do desire to learn, sir: and I hope, if you have
        occasion to use me for your own turn, you shall find
        me yare; for truly, sir, for your kindness I owe you
        a good turn.
        (4, 2, 44-46)

(20) FRIAR PETER   (falsely testifying against Isabella in accordance with the Duke's scheme)
        Blessed be your royal grace!
        I have stood by, my lord, and I have heard
        Your royal ear abused. First, hath this woman
        Most wrongfully accused your substitute,
        Who is as free from touch or soil with her
        As she from one ungot [not begotten].
        (5, 1, 137-42)

    DUKE VINCENTIO (pretending to agree with the Friar's testimony,

                asking him whether he knows `Lodowick´, who is the
                `Duke-in-disguise´)
                We did believe no less.
                Know you that Friar Lodowick that she speaks of?
                (5, 1, 142-43)

(21) LUCIO   (pointing out the coming of `Lodowick´, whom he does not like)
                My lord, here comes the rascal I spoke of; here with the provost.
                (5, 1, 279-80)
     ESCALUS (commanding Lucio not to address `Lodowick´ till
                he is granted permission to do so)
                In very good time: speak not you to him till we
                call upon you.
                (5, 1, 281-82)

(22) MARIANA (earnestly asking the Duke to let her have Angelo back as
                her husband)
                O my dear lord,
                I crave no other, nor no better man.
                (5, 1, 418-19)
   DUKE VINCENTIO (commanding Mariana to stop pleading for
                Angelo by claiming his inflexibility)
                Never crave him; we are definitive.
                (5, 1, 420)

(23) ISABELLA (urged by Mariana to help her plead for Angelo)
                Most bounteous sir,
                [Kneeling]
                Look, if it please you, on this man condemned,
                As if my brother lived: I partly think
                A due sincerity governed his deeds,
                Till he did look on me: since it is so,
                Let him not die. My brother had but justice,
                In that he did the thing for which he died:
                For Angelo,
                His act did not o'ertake his bad intent,
                And must be buried but as an intent
                That perish'd by the way: thoughts are no subjects;
                Intents but merely thoughts.
                (5, 1, 436-47)
     MARIANA Merely, my lord.
     DUKE VINCENTIO   (cruelly rejecting Isabella´s plea)
                Your suit's unprofitable; stand up, I say.
                I have bethought me of another fault.
                Provost, how came it Claudio was beheaded
                At an unusual hour?
                (5, 1, 448-51)

(24) DUKE VINCENTIO   (deciding to dismiss the Provost for his laxity)
                For which I do discharge you of your office:
                Give up your keys.

	(5, 1, 454-55)
Provost	(begging the Duke for forgiveness and pointing to his decisive role in saving Claudio's life)
	Pardon me, noble lord:
	I thought it was a fault, but knew it not;
	Yet did repent me, after more advice [deliberation];
	For testimony whereof, one in the prison,
	That should by private order else have died,
	I have reserved alive.
	(5, 1, 455-460)

(25) LUCIO   (begging the Duke not to punish him by marrying him to a prostitute)
I beseech your highness; do not marry me to a whore.
Your highness said even now, I made you a duke:
Good my lord, do not recompense me in making me a cuckold.
(5, 1, 507-9)

DUKE VINCENTIO   (swearing that Lucio shall marry a prostitute but pardoning his slanders)
Upon mine honour, thou shalt marry her.
Thy slanders I forgive; and therewithal
Remit thy other forfeits. Take him to prison;
And see our pleasure herein executed [carried out]
(5, 1, 510-13)

The Taming of the Shrew

(26) Lord   (commanding the First huntsman to look after the dogs)
Thou art a fool: if Echo were as fleet,
I would esteem him worth a dozen such.
But sup them well and look unto them all:
To-morrow I intend to hunt again.
(Induction 1, 22-5)

First Huntsman   (obediently promising to carry out the command)
I will, my lord.
(Induction 1, 26)

(27) Lord   Take him up gently and to bed with him;
And each one to his office when he wakes.
[Some bear out SLY. A trumpet sounds]
(ordering his servant to see who is playing the trumpet outside)
Sirrah, go see what trumpet 'tis that sounds:
[Exit Servingman]
Belike, some noble gentleman that means,
Travelling some journey, to repose him here.
[Re-enter Servingman]
How now! who is it?
(Induction 1, 68-73)

Servant   (deferentially telling his lord some players offer to keep him company)

		An't [if it] please your honour, players That offer service to your lordship. (Induction 1, 73-4)

(28) Lord   (questioning whether the players are going to stay for the night)
              Do you intend to stay with me tonight?
              (Induction, 1, 76)
    A Player (offering to amuse the lord)
              So please your lordship to accept our duty.
              (Induction, 1, 77)

(29) LUCENTIO   (announcing his intentions of coming to Padua,
                  complimenting his servant, Tranio, and asking
                  his mind as to what he should study)
                  Tranio, since for the great desire I had
                  To see fair Padua, nursery of arts,
                  I am arrived for fruitful Lombardy,
                  The pleasant garden of great Italy;
                  And by my father's love and leave am armed
                  With his good will and thy good company,
                  My trusty servant, well approved in all,
                  Here let us breathe and haply institute
                  A course of learning and ingenious studies.
                  Pisa renown'd for grave citizens
                  Gave me my being and my father first,
                  A merchant of great traffic through the world,
                  Vincetino come of Bentivolii.
                  Vincetino's son brought up in Florence
                  It shall become to serve all hopes conceived,
                  To deck his fortune with his virtuous deeds:
                  And therefore, Tranio, for the time I study,
                  Virtue and that part of philosophy
                  Will I apply [pursue] that treats of happiness
                  By virtue specially to be achieved.
                  Tell me thy mind; for I have Pisa left
                  And am to Padua come, as he that leaves
                  A shallow plash to plunge him in the deep
                  And with satiety seeks to quench his thirst.
                  (1, 1, 1-24)
      TRANIO   (encouraging his master in his strife for knowledge
                  and suggesting the right field of study)
                  Mi perdonato [Pardon me], gentle master mine,
                  I am in all affected [disposed] as yourself;
                  Glad that you thus continue your resolve
                  To suck the sweets of sweet philosophy.
                  Only, good master, while we do admire
                  This virtue and this moral discipline,
                  Let's be no stoics nor no stocks [blocks of woods], I pray;
                  Or so devote to Aristotle's cheques [restrictions]
                  As Ovid be an outcast quite abjured:
                  Balk logic [engage in formal arguments] with

acquaintance that you have
And practise rhetoric in your common talk;
Music and poesy use to quicken [animate] you;
The mathematics and the metaphysics,
Fall to them as you find your stomach [taste] serves you;
No profit grows where is no pleasure ta'en [taken]:
In brief, sir, study what you most affect [like].
(1, 1, 25-40)

(30) PETRUCHIO (announcing his motif for coming to Padua and ordering his servant to knock at Hortentio´s door)
Verona, for a while I take my leave,
To see my friends in Padua, but of all
My best beloved and approved friend,
Hortensio; and I trow [believe] this is his house.
Here, sirrah Grumio; knock, I say.
(1, 2, 1-5)

GRUMIO (misunderstanding Petruchio, he asks in bewilderment whom he should knock down)
Knock, sir! whom should I knock? is there man has rebused your worship?
(1, 2, 6-7)

(31) PETRUCHIO (insulting the tailor harshly for having marred the gown, but all in pretence)
O monstrous arrogance! Thou liest, thou thread, thou thimble,
Thou yard, three-quarters, half-yard, quarter, nail [one sixtieth of a yard]!
Thou flea, thou nit, thou winter-cricket thou!
Braved in mine own house with a skein of thread?
Away, thou rag, thou quantity [quantity of cloth], thou remnant;
Or I shall so bemete [beat] thee with thy yard
As thou shalt think on prating whilst thou livest!
I tell thee, I, that thou hast marr'd her gown.
(4, 3, 106-13)

Tailor (reacting innocently to Petruchio´s accusations)
Your worship is deceived; the gown is made
Just as my master had direction:
Grumio gave order how it should be done.
(4, 3, 114-16)

(32) VINCENTIO [Seeing BIONDELLO]
(shouting for Biondello, who is trying to avoid Vincentio, to come)
Come hither, crack-hemp [rogue].
(5, 1, 36)

BIONDELLO (claiming the right not to obey)
I hope I may choose [please myself or choose my master], sir.
(5, 1, 37)

Twelfth Night

(33) CURIO (asking Duke Orsino whether he would like to go hunting)

                    Will you go hunt, my lord?
                    (1, 1, 16)
        DUKE ORSINO   (abruptly asking Curio to repeat his question)
                    What, Curio?
                    (1, 1, 17)

(34) OLIVIA   (asking Cesario to speak pretending not to be Olivia)
                Speak to me; I shall answer for her.
                Your will?
                (1, 5, 139-40)
        VIOLA   (praising Olivia for her beauty and telling her how
                difficult it is for him/her to deliver his/her message)
                Most radiant, exquisite and unmatchable beauty,- Ipray
                you, tell me if this be the lady of the house, for I never saw her:
                I would be loath to cast away my speech [waste my efforts], for
                besides that it is excellently well penned, I have taken great
                pains to con it [learn it by heart]. Good beauties, let me sustain
                no scorn [suffer no derision]; I am very comptible [sensitive], even
                to the least sinister [wrong] usage.
                (1, 5, 141-6)

(35) MALVOLIO   (obediently responding to Olivia's call)
                Here, madam, at your service.
                (1, 5, 254)
        OLIVIA (telling Malvolio that Cesario left a ring behind,
                which is not true, and sending Malvolio to give him
                the ring back and tell him to stop carrying love
                messages from Orsino)
                Run after that same peevish [perverse] messenger,
                The county's [count's] man: he left this ring behind him,
                Would I or not: tell him I'll none of it.
                Desire him not to flatter [encourage] with his lord,
                Nor hold him up with hopes; I am not for him:
                If that the youth will come this way to-morrow,
                I'll give him reasons for't: hie [hasten] thee, Malvolio.
                (1, 5, 255-61)

(36) Clown   (confusedly asking Sebastian whether he
                 is not addressing Cesario)
                Will you make me believe that I am not sent for you?
                (3, 4, 1)
    SEBASTIAN   (discarding the Clown)
                Go to, go to, thou art a foolish fellow:
                Let me be clear of thee.
                (3, 4, 2-3)

(37) DUKE ORSINO   (treating Antonio as an enemy and wondering how
                he dares come to Illyria)
                Notable [Notorious] pirate! thou salt-water thief!
                What foolish boldness brought thee to their mercies,
                Whom thou, in terms so bloody and so dear [in a manner so

                    bloodthirsty and so grievous],
                    Hast made thine enemies?
                    (5, 1, 58-61)
    ANTONIO   (admitting being Orsino's enemy, defending himself against
                    the accusations brought against him, and justifying his presence
                    in the town)
                    Orsino, noble sir,
                    Be pleased that I shake off these names you give me:
                    Antonio never yet was thief or pirate,
                    Though I confess, on base and ground enough [on sufficient foundation],
                    Orsino's enemy. A witchcraft drew me hither:
                    That most ingrateful boy there by your side,
                    From the rude sea's enraged and foamy mouth
                    Did I redeem; a wrack past hope he was:
                    His life I gave him and did thereto add
                    My love, without retention or restraint,
                    All his in dedication; for his sake
                    Did I expose myself, pure [only] for his love,
                    Into the danger of this adverse [dangerous] town;
                    Drew to defend him when he was beset:
                    Where being apprehended, his false cunning,
                    Not meaning to partake with me in danger,
                    Taught him to face me out of his acquaintance [brazenly to deny he knew me],
                    And grew a twenty years removed [distant] thing
                    While one would wink; denied me mine own purse,
                    Which I had recommended [committed] to his use
                    Not half an hour before.
                    (5, 1, 61-81)

Strongly contradictory contrasts

Much Ado about Nothing

(38) HERO   (asking Margaret's opinion as to what to wear during the wedding)
                   No, pray thee, good Meg, I'll wear this.
                   (3, 4, 6)
    MARGARET   (emphasising her disagreement with Hero's
                   taste about clothes by claiming that Beatrice will say so)
                   By my troth 's not so good, and I warrant your
                   cousin will say so.
                   (3, 4, 7-8)

Measure for Measure

(39) ISABELLA (challenging Angelo by inviting him to put himself in her brother's
                       shoes)
                   Because authority, though it err like others,
                   Hath yet a kind of medicine in itself,

		That skins the vice o' the top. Go to your bosom;

                          That skins the vice o' the top. Go to your bosom;
                          Knock there, and ask your heart what it doth know
                          That's like my brother's fault: if it confess
                          A natural guiltiness such as is his,
                          Let it not sound a thought upon your tongue
                          Against my brother's life.
                          (2, 2, 138-45)
        ANGELO   (confessing his guilt when soliloquising and then bidding her farewell)
                          [Aside] She speaks, and 'tis
                          Such sense [meaning], that my sense [sensual desire] breeds with it.
                          Fare you well.
                          (2, 2, 146-47)

(40) POMPEY   (ironically calling the imprisoned Barnardine to prepare himself for execution)
                          Your friends, sir; the hangman. You must be so
                          good, sir, to rise and be put to death.
                          (4, 3, 23-24)
        BARNARDINE (vigorously refusing to be put to death)
                          [Within] Away, you rogue, away! I am sleepy.
                          (4, 3, 25)

The Taming of the Shrew

(41) KATHARINA   (humbly asking Petruchio's servant, Grumio, to have some food)
                          'Tis passing [extremely] good: I prithee let me have it.
                          (4, 3, 18)
        GRUMIO   (ridiculously depriving her of food)
                          I fear it is too choleric a meat.
                          How say you to a fat tripe finely broil'd?
                          (4, 3, 19-20)

Twelfth Night

(42) OLIVIA   (expressing her regret at the ring trick she played on Cesario and her fear that this will endanger her reputation)
                          Give me leave, beseech you. I did send,
                          After the last enchantment you did here,
                          A ring in chase of you: so did I abuse
                          Myself, my servant and, I fear me, you:
                          Under your hard construction [harsh interpretation] must I sit,
                          To force that on you, in a shameful cunning,
                          Which you knew none of yours: what might you think?
                          Have you not set mine honour at the stake
                          And baited it with all the unmuzzled thoughts
                          That tyrannous heart can think? To one of your receiving
                          Enough is shown: a cypress, not a bosom,
                          Hideth my heart. So, let me hear you speak.

	(3, 1, 96-107)
VIOLA	(expressing her pity for Olivia)
	I pity you.
	(3, 1, 108)

(43) Sir Toby   (ironically asking Malvolio how he is)
how is't with you, man?
(3, 4, 78)

MALVOLIO   (rejecting Sir Toby's salutation and harshly expressing his wish to get rid of him)
Go off; I discard you: let me enjoy my private: go off
(3, 4, 79)

Weakly Contradictory contrasts

Much Ado about Nothing

(44) DON PEDRO   (asking the musician to try out a good piece of music for Hero's wedding the following day)
Yea, marry, thou hear, Balthasar? I pray thee,
get us some excellent music; for to-morrow night we
would have it at the Lady Hero's chamber-window.
(2, 3, 76-78)

BALTHASAR   (offering the best he can play)
The best I can, my lord.
(2, 3, 79)

Measure for Measure

(45) DUKE VINCENTIO   (telling Lucio to stop interrupting him and behave
I wish you now, then; pray you,
take note of it: and when you have a business
for yourself, pray heaven you then be perfect.
5, 1, 79-81)

LUCIO   (obediently responding to the Duke's command)
I warrant your honour.
(5, 1, 82)

Twelfth Night

(46) DUKE ORSINO   (wondering at the Clown's bad advice as to their friendship)
O, you give me ill counsel.
(5, 1, 24)

Clown   (telling Orsino to forget being a duke and behave like a human being)
Put your grace in your pocket, sir, for this once,
and let your flesh and blood obey it.
(5, 1, 25-6)

Contrasts of extremity alone

Much Ado about Nothing

(47) CLAUDIO   (addressing Don Pedro to ask whether Leonato has any son)
          My liege, your highness now may do me good.
          (1, 1, 216)

    CLAUDIO   (rejecting Don Pedro's suggestion that he should go and see
          Benedick and tell him of Beatrice love)
          Never tell him, my lord: let her wear it out with good
          counsel [endure and overcome it with wise reflection].
          (2, 3, 168)

(48) LEONATO   (offering Claudio his daughter)
          Count, take of me my daughter, and with her my
          fortunes: his grace hath made the match, and an
          grace say Amen to it.
          (2, 1, 229-30)

    LEONATO   (postponing the wedding for a few days)
          Not till Monday, my dear son, which is hence a just
          seven-night [just a week]; and a time too brief, too, to have all
          things answer my mind [be as I would wish them].
          (2, 1, 271-72)

(49) DON JOHN   (asking Don Pedro to let Claudio also hear what he has to
          say about Hero's fidelity)
          If it please you: yet Count Claudio may hear; for
          what I would speak of concerns him.
          (3, 2, 63-4)

    DON JOHN   (suggesting that they should go since his plot to break up
          Claudio's engagement to Hero has been achieved)
          Come, let us go. These things, come thus to light,
          Smother her spirits up.
          (4, 1, 104-5)

(50) DOGBERR   (giving the watchmen routine instructions before they leave
          for work)
          Ha, ah, ha! Well, masters, good night: an there be
          any matter of weight chances, call up me: keep your
          fellows' counsels and your own; and good night.
          Come, neighbour.
          (3, 3, 70-72)

  a DOGBERRY   (commanding his watchmen to watch about Leonato's, for
          wedding is going to take place there)
          One word more, honest neighbours. I pray you watch
          about Signior Leonato's door; for the wedding being
          there to-morrow, there is a great coil [business] to-night.
          Adieu: be vigitant [vigilant], I beseech you.
          (3, 3, 75-77)

(51) DOGBERRY   (being complimented by Leonato (5, 1, 279), Dogberry
          Your worship speaks like a most thankful and

                  reverend youth; and I praise God for you.
                  (5, 1, 280-81)
       DOGBERRY   (requesting Leonato to punish Conrade and extravagantly
                  I leave an arrant knave with your worship; which I
                  beseech your worship to correct yourself, for the
                  example of others. God keep your worship! I wish
                  your worship well; God restore you to health! I
                  humbly give you leave to depart; and if a merry
                  meeting may be wished, God prohibit [permit] it!
                  Come, neighbour.
                  [Exeunt DOGBERRY and VERGES]
                  (5, 1, 285-89)

(52) BENEDICK   (requesting Margaret to call Beatrice)
                  Pray thee, sweet Mistress Margaret, deserve well at
                  my hands by helping me to the speech of Beatrice.
                  (5, 2, 1-2)
       BENEDICK   (advising Margaret how to deal with the 'swords')
                  If you use them, Margaret, you must put in the pikes [screws]
                  with a vice; and they are dangerous weapons for maids.
                  (5, 2, 14-15)

Measure for Measure

(53) DUKE VINCENTIO   (explaining to Friar Thomas that his intention to
                  disguise himself is not for his own entertainment but for a more
                  serious aim)
                  No, holy father; throw away that thought;
                  Believe not that the dribbling dart of love
                  Can pierce a complete bosom. Why I desire thee
                  To give me secret harbour, hath a purpose
                  More grave and wrinkled [wise] than the aims and ends
                  Of burning youth.
                  (1, 3, 1-6)
       DUKE VINCENTIO   (acknowledging his responsibility for having giving
                  his people to much liberty, dismissing the idea of harming his
                  people, and humbly requesting Friar Thomas to assist him in his
                  disguise)
                  I do fear, too dreadful [inspiring with terror of punishment]:
                  Sith 'twas my fault to give the people scope,
                  'Twould be my tyranny to strike and gall them
                  For what I bid them do: for we bid this be done,
                  When evil deeds have their permissive pass
                  And not the punishment. Therefore indeed, my father,
                  I have on Angelo imposed the office;
                  Who may, in the ambush of my name, strike home,
                  And yet my nature [person] never in the fight
                  To do in slander. And to behold his sway [observe his rule],
                  I will, as 'twere a brother of your order,
                  Visit both prince and people: therefore, I prithee,
                  Supply me with the habit and instruct me

How I may formally [in outward appearance and manner] in person bear me
Like a true friar. More reasons for this action
At our more leisure shall I render you;
Only, this one: Lord Angelo is precise;
Stands at a guard [keeps up his defence] with
envy [with malice]; scarce confesses.
That his blood flows, or that his appetite
Is more to bread than stone: hence shall we see,
If power change purpose, what our seemers be.
[Exeunt]
(1, 3, 35-55)

(54) LUCIO (describing the cruelty of the Duke's deputy, Angelo, to Isabella and urging her to go to see him and beg him spare her brother's life)
This is the point.
The duke is very strangely gone from hence;
Bore many gentlemen, myself being one,
In hand and hope of action [military action]: but we do learn
By those that know the very nerves [the means of acting, using strength] of state,
His givings-out [what he said publicly] were of an infinite distance
From his true-meant design. Upon his place,
And with full line of his authority,
Governs Lord Angelo; a man whose blood
Is very snow-broth [melted snow]; one who never feels
The wanton stings and motions [urges] of the sense,
But doth rebate [reduce] and blunt his natural edge
With profits of the mind, study and fast.
He-to give fear to use and liberty [licentiousness which has become customary],
Which have for long run by the hideous law,
As mice by lions-hath pick'd out an act,
Under whose heavy sense [severe meaning] your brother's life
Falls into forfeit: he arrests him on it [under it];
And follows close the rigour of the statute,
To make him an example. All hope is gone,
Unless you have the grace by your fair prayer
To soften Angelo: and that's my pith of business (the essence of my errand)
'Twixt you and your poor brother.
(1, 4, 49-71)

LUCIO (demanding from Isabella more engagement in her plea for her brother's life)
[Aside to ISABELLA] Give't not o'er so: to him
again, entreat him;
Kneel down before him, hang upon his gown:
You are too cold; if you should need a pin [a trifle],
You could not with more tame a tongue desire it:
To him, I say!
(2, 2, 44-48)

(55) ISABELLA (explaining to Angelo her dilemma between loving her
brother and disliking his crime)
There is a vice that most I do abhor,
And most desire should meet the blow of justice;
For which I would not plead, but that I must;
For which I must not plead, but that I am
At war 'twixt will and will not.
2, 30-34)

ISABELLA (pleading Angelo to save her brother's life)
I have a brother is condemn'd to die:
I do beseech you, let it be his fault,
And not my brother.
(2, 2, 35-37)

(56) CLAUDIO (begging his sister to save him by accepting Angelo's
demand and sleep with him)
Sweet sister, let me live:
What sin you do to save a brother's life,
Nature dispenses with [pardons] the deed so far
That it becomes a virtue.
(3, 1, 133-36)

CLAUDIO (calling Isabella back when she is leaving the prison after her
furious refusal to surround her chastity)
Nay, hear me, Isabel.
(3, 1, 148)

(57) DUKE VINCENTIO (asking the Provost to conceal him during the
encounter between Isabella and her brother, thereby enabling him
to overhear them)
Bring me to hear them speak, where I may be concealed.
(3, 1, 52

DUKE VINCENTIO (requesting the Provost to delay Claudio's
execution)
More of him anon. There is written in your brow, provost,
honesty and constancy: if I read it not truly, my ancient skill
beguiles me; but, in the boldness of my cunning, I will lay myself
in hazard. Claudio, whom here you have warrant to execute, is
no greater forfeit [no worse a criminal] to the law than Angelo
who hath sentenced him. To make you understand this in a
manifested effect [clear demonstration], I crave
but four days' respite; for the which you are to do me both
a present [immediate] and a dangerous courtesy [service].
(4, 2, 135-42)

The Taming of the Shrew

(58) Lord (asking his household to make Christopher Sly believe that he is a
noble lord woken up from a long sleep)
O monstrous beast! how like a swine he lies!
Grim death, how foul and loathsome is thine image!

                    Sirs, I will practise [play a trick on] on this drunken man.
                    What think you, if he were convey'd to bed?
                    Wrapp'd in sweet [perfumed] clothes, rings put upon his fingers,
                    A most delicious banquet by his bed,
                    And brave [finely dressed] attendants near him when he wakes,
                    Would not the beggar then forget himself?
                    (Induction 1, 30-7)
    Lord   (ordering his servants to put the trick into practice)
                    Take him up gently and to bed with him;
                    And each one to his office [perform his role] when he wakes.
                    (Some bear out SLY. A trumpet sounds)
                    (Induction 1, 68-9)

(59) HORTENSIO   (suggesting cooperation with his rival in Bianca's love
                           in that they should find a husband for Bianca's shrewish
                           sister, Katharina)
                    So will I, Signior Gremio: but a word, I pray.
                    Though the nature of our quarrel yet never brooked
                    parle [allowed negotiations between us], know now, upon
                    advice [reflection], it toucheth [concerns] us both,
                    that we may yet again have access to our fair
                    mistress and be happy rivals in Bianca's love, to
                    labour and effect one thing specially.
                    (1, 1, 111-5)
    HORTENSIO   (trying to persuade Gremio that someone may be interested
                           in Katharina's fortune in spite of her shrewish character)
                    Tush, Gremio, though it pass your patience and mine
                    to endure her loud alarums [scoldings], why, man, there be good
                    fellows in the world, an a man could light on them,

                    would take her with all faults, and money enough.
                    (1, 1, 122-25)

(60) PETRUCHIO   (asking Hortensio to find a rich woman for him whatever
                           her faults may be)
                    Signior Hortensio, 'twixt such friends as we
                    Few words suffice; and therefore, if thou know
                    One rich enough to be Petruchio's wife,
                    As wealth is burden of my wooing dance,
                    Be she as foul as was Florentius' love,
                    As old as Sibyl and as curst and shrewd
                    As Socrates' Xanthippe, or a worse,
                    She moves me not, or not removes, at least,
                    Affection's edge [the intensity of passion or desire] in me,
                    were she as rough
                    As are the swelling Adriatic seas:
                    I come to wive it wealthily in Padua;
                    If wealthily, then happily in Padua.
                    (1, 2, 62-73)
    PETRUCHIO   (in an aside he demands from Hortensio to get the tailor
                         paid without letting Katharina overhear him)

                [Aside] Hortensio, say thou wilt see the tailor paid.
                (to Tailor) Go take it hence; be gone, and say no more.
                (4, 3, 158-159)

(61) HORTENSIO   (requesting Petruchio to assist him in his disguise as a music-teacher so as to gain access to Bianca to court her)
Now shall my friend Petruchio do me grace,
And offer me disguised in sober robes
To old Baptista as a schoolmaster
Well seen [qualified] in music, to instruct Bianca;
That so I may, by this device, at least
Have leave and leisure to make love [speak of love] to her
And unsuspected court her by herself.
(1, 2, 125)

    HORTENSIO   (telling Petruchio to confess being defeated by Tranio in argument)
Confess, confess, hath he not hit you here?
(5, 2, 59)

(62) TRANIO   (offering to house the pedant and expecting from him to play the role of Vincentio before Baptista in return)
To save your life in this extremity,
This favour will I do you for his sake;
And think it not the worst of an your fortunes
That you are like to Sir Vincentio.
His name and credit [status] shall you undertake [Adopt],
And in my house you shall be friendly lodged:
Look that you take upon you [play your role] as you should;
You understand me, sir: so shall you stay
Till you have done your business in the city:
If this be courtesy, sir, accept of it.
(4, 2, 102-11)

    TRANIO   (asking the pedant to be perfect in his disguise without panic)
'Tis well; and hold your own [keep up your role], in any case [circumstance],
With such austerity as longeth to a father.
(4, 4, 6-7)

Twelfth Night

(63) VIOLA   (complimenting Antonio for his good qualities and requesting him to assist her in her disguise as a page boy so as to gain access to Duke Orsino's milieu)
There is a fair behavior in thee, captain;
And though that nature with a beauteous wall
Doth oft close in pollution, yet of thee
I will believe thou hast a mind that suits
With this thy fair and outward character.
I prithee, and I'll pay thee bounteously,
Conceal me what I am [conceal that I am a woman], and be my aid

112

>   For such disguise as haply shall become [suit]
>   The form of my intent. I'll serve this duke:
>   Thou shall present me as an eunuch to him:
>   It may be worth thy pains; for I can sing
>   And speak to him in many sorts of music
>   That will allow me very worth his service [prove me worthy to serve him].
>   What else may hap to time I will commit;
>   Only shape thou thy silence to my wit.
>   (1, 2, 47-61)

    VIOLA   (thanking Antonio for his readiness to help her and asking him to lead the way)

> I thank thee: lead me on.
> (1, 2, 51-64)

(64) DUKE ORSINO (expressing his sympathy for Cesario and sending him to carry a love message to Olivia)

> (*To Curio and Attendants*) Stand you a while aloof [aside], Cesario,
> Thou know'st no less but all; I have unclasp'd
> To thee the book even of my secret soul:
> Therefore, good youth, address thy gait [go] unto her;
> Be not denied access, stand at her doors,
> And tell them, there thy fixed foot shall grow
> Till thou have audience.
> (1, 4, 11-7)

    DUKE ORSINO   (telling Cesario which women to choose and pointing to women's sensitivity)

> Then let thy love be younger than thyself,
> Or thy affection cannot hold the bent [keep its intensity];
> For women are as roses, whose fair flower
> Being once display'd, doth fall that very hour.
> (2, 4, 34-37)

(65) OLIVIA (impatiently asking Cesario to deliver his/her message, her suspicion being aroused by Cesario's politeness)

> Sure, you have some hideous matter to deliver, when
> the courtesy of it is so fearful. Speak your office.
> (1, 5, 170-71)

    OLIVIA   (bidding Cesario stop delivering Orsino's love messages and speaking of him)

> O, by your leave, I pray you,
> I bade you never speak again of him:
> But, would you undertake another suit,
> I had rather hear you to solicit that
> Than music from the spheres.
> (3, 1, 91-94)

(66) MALVOLIO (calling for the Clown)

> Fool, fool, fool, I say!

                    (4, 2, 87)
MALVOLIO   (asking the Clown to take a letter to Olivia, who
            mistakenly imprisoned him, and assuring him that it
            would be of great benefit for him)
            By this hand, I am. Good fool, some ink, paper and
            light; and convey what I will set down to my lady:
            it shall advantage thee more than ever the bearing
            of letter did.
            (4, 2, 93-5)

Contrasts of distance (*D*) as affect

Much Ado about Nothing

(67) LEONATO   (postponing the wedding for a few days)
                 Not till Monday, my dear son, which is hence a just
                 seven-night; and a time too brief, too, to have all
                 things answer my mind.
                 (2, 1, 271-72)
     LEONATO   (contemptuously accusing Claudio of being a deceiver and
                 declaring that he is not frightened of him)
                 Marry, thou dost wrong me; thou dissembler, thou:
                 Nay, never lay thy hand upon thy sword;
                 I fear thee not.
                 (5, 1, 53-55)

(68) HERO   (shouting to Margaret to be ashamed of herself)
                 Fie upon thee! art not ashamed?
                 (3, 4, 21)
     HERO   (asking Margaret, Ursula, and her cousin, Beatrice, to help her get
                 dressed for the wedding)
                 Help to dress me, good coz, good Meg, good Ursula.
                 (3, 4, 71)

(69) CLAUDIO (accusing Hero of infidelity)
             Out on thee! Seeming! [I've had enough of seeming] I will write
             against it:
             You seem to me as Dian [goddess of chastity] in her orb,
             As chaste as is the bud ere it be blown [fully open];
             But you are more intemperate in your blood
             Than Venus, or those pampered [overfed and indulgent in luxury]
             animals
             That rage in savage sensuality.
             (4, 1, 50-55)
     CLAUDIO (taking back his accusations and expressing his love for Hero)
             Sweet Hero! now thy image doth appear
             In the rare semblance that I loved it first.
             (5, 1, 220-21)

(70) BENEDICK   (challenging Claudio to a duel as revenge for Hero)
                 [Aside to CLAUDIO] You are a villain; I jest not:

>   I will make it good how you dare, with what you
>   dare, and when you dare. Do me right, or I will
>   protest your cowardice. You have killed a sweet
>   lady, and her death shall fall heavy on you. Let me
>   hear from you.
>   (5, 1, 137-40)
>
> BENEDICK   (happily inviting Claudio to a dance)
>   Come, come, we are friends, let's have a dance ere we are
>   married, that we may lighten our own hearts, and our wives' heels.
>   (5, 4, 111-12)

(71) CLAUDIO   (refusing to argue with Leonato)
>   Away! I will not have to do with you.
>   (5, 1, 77)
>
> CLAUDIO   (deferentially accepting Leonato's offer to marry Hero's niece)
>   O noble sir,
>   Your over-kindness doth wring tears from me!
>   I do embrace your offer; and dispose
>   For henceforth of poor Claudio.
>   (5, 1, 259-62)

(72) DON PEDRO   (offering his hand modestly instead of leading the way as
>   Your hand, Leonato; we will go together.
>   (1, 1, 118)
>
> DON PEDRO   (contemptuously disagreeing with Leonato)
>   You say not right, old man.
>   (5, 1, 73)

Measure for Measure

(73) DUKE VINCENTIO   (complimenting Angelo for his good qualities
>   and appointing him as a deputy during his absence)
>   Angelo,
>   There is a kind of character in thy life,
>   That to the observer [close remarker] doth thy history [personal record]
>   Fully unfold. Thyself and thy belongings [qualities]
>   Are not thine own so proper [so much thy own property] as to waste
>   Thyself upon thy virtues, they on thee.
>   Heaven doth with us as we with torches do,
>   Not light them for themselves; for if our virtues
>   Did not go forth of us, 'twere all alike
>   As if we had them not. Spirits are not finely
>   touched [affected with fine emotions]
>   But to fine issues [morally fine causes or deeds], nor Nature never lends
>   The smallest scruple [a very small unit or weight] of her excellence
>   But, like a thrifty goddess, she determines
>   Herself the glory of a creditor,
>   Both thanks and use. But I do bend my speech

>
> To one that can my part in him advertise;
> Hold [hold your peace or silence] therefore, Angelo:
> In our remove [absence] be thou at full ourself [in every respect
> our deputy];
> Mortality and mercy in Vienna
> Live in thy tongue and heart: old Escalus,
> Though first in question, is thy secondary.
> Take thy commission.
> (1, 1, 26-47)

DUKE VINCENTIO (having unmasked Angelo, who begs for the grace of death (cf. 5, 1, 359-67), the Duke denies him this and orders him marry his cast off fianceé, Mariana)
> For this new-married man approaching here,
> Whose salt [lecherous] imagination yet hath wrong'd
> Your well defended honour, you must pardon
> For Mariana's sake: but as he adjudged [condemned] your brother,
> Being criminal, in double violation
> Of sacred chastity and of promise-breach
> Thereon dependent, for your brother's life,
> The very mercy of the law cries out
> Most audible, even from his proper tongue,
> 'An Angelo for Claudio, death for death!'
> Haste still pays [recompenses] haste, and leisure answers leisure;
> Like doth quit like, and MEASURE still FOR MEASURE.
> Then, Angelo, thy fault's thus manifested;
> Which, though thou wouldst deny, denies thee vantage.
> We do condemn thee to the very block
> Where Claudio stoop'd to death, and with like haste.
> Away with him!
> (5, 1, 393-409)

(74) ISABELLA (asking God's favour for Angelo when taking leave of him after their first encounter, which ends with Isabella's optimism that Angelo will reconsider his judgement and save her brother's head)
> Heaven keep your honour safe!
> (2, 2, 162)

ISABELLA (threatening to unmask Angelo when he promises to save her brother's life if she sleeps with him)
> Ha! little honour to be much believed,
> And most pernicious purpose! Seeming, seeming!
> I will proclaim thee, Angelo; look for't:
> Sign me a present pardon for my brother,
> Or with an outstretch'd throat I'll tell the world aloud
> What man thou art.
> (2, 4, 150-55)

(75) LUCIO (telling 'Friar Lodowick', whose true identity he ignores, that he is not well informed about the Duke)
> O, sir, you are deceived.
> (3, 2, 108)

LUCIO	(turning on 'Friar Lodowick', scornfully accusing him of slandering the Duke when 'Friar Lodowick' threatens to denounce him)
	O thou damnable fellow! Did not I pluck thee by the nose for thy speeches?
	(5, 1, 334-35)

The Taming of the Shrew

(76) TRANIO   (claiming the right to court Bianca as well)
Why, sir, I pray, are not the streets as free
For me as for you?
(1, 2, 225-26)

     TRANIO   (criticising his rival for his old age)
Graybeard, thy love doth freeze.
(2, 1, 327)

(77) GREMIO   (contemptuously criticising Lucentio/Tranio, who bids higher for Bianca)
Adieu, good neighbour.
[Exit BAPTISTA]
Now I fear thee not:
Sirrah young gamester, your father were a fool
To give thee all, and in his waning age
Set foot under thy table [live on your charity]: tut, a toy [piece of nonsense]!
An old Italian fox is not so kind, my boy.
(2, 1, 388-92)

     GREMIO   (describing to Lucentio/Tranio Petruchio's strange behaviour before the priest when marrying Katharina)
Tut, she's a lamb, a dove, a fool to him!
I'll tell you, Sir Lucentio: when the priest
Should ask, if Katharina should be his wife,
'Ay, by gogs-wouns,' [God's wounds] quoth he; and swore so loud,
That, all-amazed, the priest let fall the book;
And, as he stoop'd again to take it up,
The mad-brain'd bridegroom took him such a cuff
That down fell priest and book and book and priest:
'Now take them up,' quoth he, 'if any list.'
(3, 2, 147-55)

Twelfth Night

(78) DUKE ORSINO   (inviting Cesario/Viola to come and describe to him/her the song they had the previous night)
O, fellow, come, the song we had last night.
Mark it, Cesario, it is old and plain [artless];
The spinsters and the knitters in the sun
And the free maids that weave their thread with bones

>   Do use to chant it: it is silly sooth [simple truth],
>   And dallies with the innocence of love,
>   Like the old age.
>   (2, 4, 40-46)

DUKE ORSINO (mistakenly and contemptuously thinking that Cesario/Viola is Olivia's husband)
>   Her husband, sirrah!
>   (5, 1, 134)

(79) DUKE ORSINO (greeting Olivia when he comes personally to express his love for her)
>   Gracious Olivia,-
>   (5, 1, 94)

DUKE ORSINO (expressing his disappointment with Olivia, who does not share his love)
>   What, to perverseness? you uncivil [uncivilised] lady,
>   To whose ingrate and unauspicious [thankless and unpropitious] altars
>   My soul the faithfull'st offerings hath breathed out
>   That e'er devotion tender'd! What shall I do?
>   (5, 1, 101-4)

(80) MALVOLIO (wondering at Olivia's approval of the Clown and contemptuously describing the Clown's companionship)
>   I marvel your ladyship takes delight in such a
>   barren rascal: I saw him put down the other day
>   with an ordinary fool that has no more brain
>   than a stone. Look you now, he's out of his guard [used up his tricks of defence]
>   already; unless you laugh and minister occasion to
>   him, he is gagged. I protest, I take these wise men,
>   that crow so at these set kind of fools, no better
>   than the fools' zanies.
>   (1, 5, 67-72)

MALVOLIO (the imprisoned Malvolio is begging the Clown to have something to write with and assuring him that he is not mad)
>   Good fool, help me to some light and some paper: I
>   tell thee, I am as well in my wits as any man in Illyria.
>   (4, 2, 90-91).

Abdelaziz Bouchara obtained his Ph.D. from the university of Heidelberg in 2001. He is presently Professor of linguistics and business German at the University of Casablanca. Current interests are politeness theory, intercultural communication and globalization. Bouchara is the author of *Höflichkeitsformen in der Interaktion zwischen Deutschen und Arabern: Ein Beitrag zur interkulturellen Kommunikation* (RGL/235, Niemeyer).

Printed in Great Britain
by Amazon